ANNOTATED TEACHE[R]

USING PRIMARY SOURCES

Level C

with Document-Based Questions

GLOBE FEARON

Pearson Learning Group

REVIEWERS

We would like to thank the following educators, who provided valuable comments and suggestions during the development of this book:

Robert E. Arons, Miami Dade County Public Schools Educational Alternative
  Outreach Program, Miami, Florida
Floyd Kessler, Queens College, City University of New York, Flushing, New York
Tamika Matheson, Paul Robeson High School, Brooklyn, New York

The following people have contributed to the development of this product:
Art and Design: Eileen Brantner, Kathy Ellison, Salita Mehta, Jim O'Shea
Editorial: Elaine Fay, Jane Petlinski, Tara Walters
Manufacturing: Nathan Kinney
Marketing: Katie Erezuma
Production: Irene Belinsky, Karen Edmonds, Jeff Engel, Cheryl Golding
Publishing Operations: Thomas Daning, Christine Guido, Richetta Lobban, Kate Matracia

IMAGE CREDITS

All photography © Pearson Education, Inc. (PEI) unless otherwise specifically noted.

Cover: *t.l.* © Réunion des Musées Nationaux/Art Resource, NY; *t.r.* The Art Archive/Dagli Orti; *m.l.* © The British Museum; *m.r.* Picture Desk, Inc./The Kobal Collection; *b.* Digital Vision Ltd. 22: The Art Archive/Eileen Tweedy. 24: The Granger Collection. 26: Bruce Beattie/Dayton Beach Morning Journal. 28: Philadelphia Business Journal. 30: © John Pritchett/Pritchett Cartoons. 46: Bundesarchiv. 50: © Burstein Collection/Corbis. 58: The Art Archive/Dagli Orti. 60: © The British Museum. 62: © Bettmann/Corbis. 64: Schalkwijk/Art Resource, NY. 66: © Alanari/Art Resource, NY. 74: The Art Archive/Jarrold Publishing. 90: Franklin D. Roosevelt Presidential Library. 95: Picture Desk, Inc./ The Kobal Collection. 96: © Corbis. 98: AP/Wide World Photo. 102: *t.* © Werner Forman/Art Resource, NY; *b.* © Réunion des Musées Nationaux/Art Resource, NY

TEXT ACKNOWLEDGMENTS

12: From *Codex Justinianus*, Book I. 34: From *The Annals*, Book XV, by Tacitus. 36: "The Book of Routes and Realms" by Abu Ubaydallah al-Bakri from *Corpus of Early Arabic Sources for West African History*. J.F.P. Hopkins, translator and N. Levtzion and J.F.P. Hopkins eds. Cambridge: Cambridge University Press, 1981. Reprinted with the permission of Cambridge University Press. 38: From *Five Letters of Cortez to the Emperor* by Hernando Cortez. J. Bayard Morris, translator. Copyright © 1969 by J. Bayard Morris. Used by permission of W.W. Norton Co. 40: From *Emperor of China* by Jonathan D. Spence, copyright © 1974 by Jonathan D. Spence. Used by permission of Alfred A. Knopf, a division of Random House, Inc. 52: From "Miss Earhart Forced Down at Sea, Howland Isle Fears; Coast Guard Begins Search." Reprinted with permission of The Associated Press. 54: From "At China's Ministry of Truth, History Is Quickly Rewritten" by Richard Bernstein. *The New York Times*, July 12, 1989. Copyright © 1989 by The New York Times Company. Reprinted with permission. 105: "Declaration of Israel's Independence 1948" from www.Yale.edu. Reprinted with permission. 106: "Ayan: Long Journey to the United States" from *Teenage Refugees From Somalia Speak Out*, Ikram Hussein, ed. Copyright © 1997 by The Rosen Publishing Group, Inc. Reprinted with permission.
NOTE: Every effort has been made to locate the copyright owner of material reprinted in this book. Omissions brought to our attention will be corrected in subsequent printings.

ISBN 0-13-024434-1

Printed in the United States of America

1 2 3 4 5 6 7 8 9 10   07 06 05 04 03

Globe
Fearon
Pearson Learning Group

1-800-321-3106
www.pearsonlearning.com

Contents

About Primary Sources

What are primary sources?

Primary sources are materials produced at specific periods in history. These materials are created by a witness or participant of an event and recorded during or after the event took place. For example, historical documents, such as the Code of Hammurabi, are primary sources. Primary sources also include objects, images, statistical data, and audio recordings.

Using Primary Sources has representations of the following types of primary sources:

- ◆ Historical documents
- ◆ Political cartoons
- ◆ Firsthand accounts
- ◆ Posters and newspapers
- ◆ Photographs, art, and artifacts
- ◆ Maps
- ◆ Informational graphics

What are secondary sources?

Secondary sources are materials based on primary sources, such as reference books and historical commentaries. These sources are removed from the real event. They are interpretations of what historians and other experts know about a topic.

Why study primary sources?

Primary sources empower students by allowing them to examine evidence firsthand—or before it has been retold from another perspective. As a result, students begin to view more traditional sources of historical information, such as their world history textbook, as only one interpretation of a set of events. History, therefore, becomes a process in which they can see themselves as active participants.

It is important to note, however, that primary sources cannot provide people with *all* the answers to historical questions. Different types of primary sources yield different types of information about the past. For example, a World War II propaganda poster can teach people about the need to rally homeland support for the war. However, it cannot teach what caused the war or how the war was won. Therefore, primary sources are best used in conjunction with other primary and secondary sources to help students develop a broad perspective on a topic.

What skills do my students use when analyzing primary sources?

Primary-source materials measure students' ability to

- ◆ Recognize how point of view affects evidence, including their own presuppositions and values.

- ◆ Analyze the motives and intended audience of the originator of the primary source.

- ◆ Interpret historical sources and recognize what contradictions and other limitations exist within a given source.

- ◆ Analyze and evaluate contemporary sources.

- ◆ Compare, contrast, and synthesize multiple perspectives.

- ◆ Participate in the process of history through debate with teachers and classmates about the interpretation of sources.

Where can my students find primary-source materials?

Primary sources can be found in a person's own home as well as in public and online communities. At home, students can find primary sources such as birth certificates, cookbooks, catalogs, or song lyrics. Historical groups, preservation societies, and museums also serve as excellent starting points for students looking for primary-source materials. Furthermore, many Web sites, such as the Library of Congress's National Archives, provide students with direct links to historical documents, photographs, political cartoons, and recordings.

About Document-Based Questions

What are document-based questions?

Document-based questions (DBQs) pertain to primary sources, such as historical documents, political cartoons, advertisements, firsthand accounts, letters, photographs, artifacts, and paintings; or to secondary sources, such as charts, graphs, and timelines. These document-based questions are frequently found in textbooks and on standardized tests. They measure students' ability to analyze and synthesize multiple perspectives and sources on relevant social studies issues and topics.

What skills do my students use to answer document-based questions?

Document-based questions challenge students to

- Interpret, analyze, synthesize, and evaluate information.

- Make comparisons and analogies.

- Apply what they already know to new information.

- Examine issues from various points of view.

- Draw conclusions.

- Focus on critical-thinking skills.

How are document-based questions relevant to my students today?

By analyzing and answering document-based questions about a variety of primary sources, students will be able to

- Better understand differing points of view on important historical and current issues.

- Make informed decisions about issues that concern themselves and others.

- Interpret information provided in newspapers, magazines, and other publications.

- Take positions on issues or problems and support their conclusions.

- Develop informed citizenship skills.

- Find out more about our world's history and how it relates to them today.

About Standardized Tests

What are some current national trends in social studies education?

Standards developed by the National Council for the Social Studies (NCSS) emphasize "achieving academic excellence by applying knowledge, skills, and civic values to civic participation." One of the skills required by NCSS is information processing, which includes recognizing, identifying, describing, explaining, interpreting, applying, analyzing, comparing, and evaluating information.

How are my students evaluated in social studies on standardized tests?

Most states now require students to read and analyze documents in their state assessments. As a result, document-based questions are appearing in more and more of these standardized examinations. These questions are used to assess students' ability to analyze different types of primary- and secondary-source documents and to use the documents to interpret, clarify, analyze, and evaluate historical events from multiple perspectives.

What types of document-based questions will students encounter on standardized tests?

The format of document-based questions can vary from state to state and from test to test. Often, multiple-choice questions and short-answer—or constructed-response—questions are based on a specific primary-source document.

Document-based questions may also be used in the essay portion of a standardized test. Here, the emphasis is on students' ability to analyze historical data gleaned from a series of documents to evaluate a specific historical period, event, topic, or theme. For example, students may be asked to view and answer three or four questions about a painting, a photograph, a code of laws, and a speech relating to world leaders. Then, an essay question requires students to incorporate information from this series of documents, as well as from their overall knowledge of history, to draw broader conclusions about the qualities of a leader.

How will *Using Primary Sources* help prepare my students for standardized tests?

Your world history textbook most likely includes primary-source documents as part of its core curriculum and may contain a few lessons on analyzing these documents. *Using Primary Sources* supplements a core world history text by providing in-depth instruction on the different kinds of primary-source documents as well as ample practice opportunities necessary to reinforce and enhance skill development.

The question formats in *Using Primary Sources* mirror those on most standardized tests, helping students to familiarize themselves with the types of questions they will encounter on a test. The test tips in each chapter provide practical strategies for students to use in a test situation to ensure greater success.

Program Overview

Using Primary Sources provides solutions for today's social studies classroom.

Teachers and students face unique challenges in today's classroom. Students must live up to rigorous academic standards and are required to demonstrate proficiency on standardized tests. As educators in diverse classrooms, you must help prepare students who have a wide range of learning styles and ability levels to meet these requirements.

To help students prepare for social studies tests at the school, state, and national levels, *Using Primary Sources* provides clear, concise instruction for analyzing various types of documents in a consistent and predictable format.

The Student Edition

The Student Edition of *Using Primary Sources* provides instruction that is accessible and relevant to students. There are ample practice opportunities that help students prepare for and succeed on standardized tests.

◆ Primary-Source Documents Are Fully Covered

As you scan the contents on pages iii and iv, you will notice the comprehensive coverage of primary sources, including historical documents, political cartoons, posters, newspapers, firsthand accounts, photographs, art, artifacts, maps, and informational graphics. Your students will encounter many or all of these types of documents on standardized tests.

◆ Model Lessons Provide Sound Instruction

Each chapter begins with a four-page Model Lesson that provides students with the necessary skills to analyze and synthesize the information found in each primary source.

◆ Here's the Skill

This section of the Model Lesson introduces the primary source, telling *what* it is and *when* it was created.

◆ Here's Why

Oftentimes, students are not sure *why* they are learning a skill or studying about a particular topic or issue. This section gives students a purpose for reading and explains why a particular primary source is relevant to their lives today.

◆ A Snapshot From History

Before your students answer questions about a primary source, they are given a historical context in which to place it. *A Snapshot From History* is a brief summary that provides background information for the primary-source document. In addition, key vocabulary words appear in boldface in the text and are defined in a *Terms to Know* box.

◆ Here's How

This section of the Model Lesson provides a step-by-step strategy for analyzing the specific type of primary source. On the first page, students view a primary-source document with callout boxes that highlight key features of the document and tips for analyzing them.

Then, students follow a three-step strategy to reinforce their understanding:

1. Read and Study

This section provides a review of the strategy presented in the callout boxes on the previous page.

2. Ask Yourself Questions

In this section, students are asked to go back to the document that they have viewed and apply the strategy to it. The questions provided are similar to those they may encounter on standardized tests.

3. Put It All Together

This section allows students to synthesize what they have studied in the Model Lesson and practice their essay-writing skills.

◆ Ample Practice Reinforces Skills

In each chapter, students are given four opportunities to practice working with a particular type of primary source. These primary sources address a variety of people, events, and historical periods.

Like the Model Lesson, each practice begins with *A Snapshot From History* and calls out the *Terms to Know*. Then, students draw from their knowledge of social studies, their world history textbook, and the content in the *Snapshot* to answer questions.

The practice questions are in either a constructed-response or multiple-choice format. A *Test Tip* in each chapter provides a practical strategy that students can use in a test situation. At the end of each practice, an essay prompt requires that students apply their understanding of the information presented in the primary source to answer a broader question. *Essay Writing Tips* guide students through the process of writing an essay.

◆ Activities Add Relevance

At the end of each chapter, students will engage in a hands-on activity that brings each primary source to life. Activities such as drawing a political cartoon, constructing a map, or writing a firsthand account help students recognize the purpose and relevance of each type of document.

◆ Practice Tests Prepare Students for Standardized Assessment

Using Primary Sources contains two tests to help students prepare for standardized assessment. Students are provided with directions, a historical context, and the essay prompt before they encounter the documents.

Part A of each test consists of a series of six primary-source documents about a theme in world history. *Background Notes* provide information about each primary source. Each document is then followed by one or two constructed-response questions.

Part B is the essay portion of the test. Students are again given the directions and the essay prompt. A graphic organizer is also provided to help students plan their essays.

◆ Essay Topics Provide Practice for Tests

Students are given three essay topics from which to practice their essay-writing skills. Students are encouraged to draw on their knowledge of world issues and events when writing their essays.

◆ Glossary and Index Provide Access to Key Information

The glossary contains all of the *Terms to Know* with their definitions and the page numbers on which they appear.

An index helps students find specific topics and primary-source documents.

◆ *How to Prepare for a Test* Unlocks the Mystery of Standardized Tests

How to Prepare for a Test provides instruction in taking standardized tests. Students are taught successful tips and strategies for answering multiple-choice and constructed-response questions.

◆ *How to Write an Essay* Helps Organize Students' Thoughts

Using Primary Sources teaches students how to write an essay for standardized tests. *How to Write an Essay* reviews the purpose and importance of writing a good essay. It also includes a breakdown of the parts of an essay and an explanation of the writing process.

The Annotated Teacher's Edition

This Annotated Teacher's Edition contains each page of the Student Edition with answers to all questions at point of use. In addition, the following items are included:

- ◆ Annotated Teacher's Edition contents pages
- ◆ About Primary Sources
- ◆ About Document-Based Questions
- ◆ About Standardized Tests
- ◆ Program Overview
- ◆ Essay Writing in Social Studies
- ◆ Sample Document-Based Question Essays
- ◆ Generic Scoring Rubric: Essay
- ◆ Generic Scoring Rubric: Constructed Response
- ◆ Generic Scoring Rubric: Activity

Essay Writing in Social Studies

How can I help my students become fluent writers in social studies?

It is no mystery that the best way to master any subject matter is to practice. Because writing is an especially complex process that involves a wide range of critical thinking and language skills, students need frequent practice to become fluent, articulate writers. Fluent writers in social studies demonstrate the ability to organize thoughts, express ideas and opinions clearly, and support those ideas and opinions with factual evidence.

The Writing Process

Remind students that writing is a process comprised of a series of steps or stages. Effective writers take the time to plan, draft, revise, and edit their work before it is considered finished. This is true even when time is limited, as in a test-taking situation. The more comfortable students are with each stage of the writing process, the more efficiently they will use their time to construct effective test essays.

Prewriting. In this planning stage writers

- Decide on a topic. If the topic is given to them in an essay prompt, students might want to rewrite the prompt in their own words or circle key words to be sure they understand the assignment.

- Organize ideas. Graphic organizers such as idea webs, outlines, KWL charts, and Venn diagrams are helpful tools students can use to organize their thoughts. See page xii for a fuller explanation of graphic organizers.

- Take notes. Remind students that on many essay tests, they will be provided with information that they must incorporate into their essays. Conversely, they might also be expected to generate their own ideas or draw from their prior knowledge. Jotting down notes in the margin as they read or study is an effective prewriting strategy.

Writing. In the writing, or drafting, stage writers

- Consider their audience and purpose for writing. Remind students that in a test-taking situation, teachers are the audience and that demonstrating an understanding of content is the purpose.

- Organize ideas into complete thoughts. Encourage students to use complete sentences and to put related ideas into paragraphs.

- Write freely without editing. Tell students to rely on the plan they created in the prewriting stage to create their first draft. They may revise their ideas and edit their work later. In a test-taking situation, it is a good idea for students to leave extra space between lines for later revisions and edits.

Revising. The revision stage is when writers

- Read the first draft several times to be sure it answers all aspects of the essay prompt.

- Check that each paragraph contains a main idea and supporting details.

- Improve the draft by adding supporting details and facts, deleting unrelated or extraneous information, and reordering ideas into a more logical flow.

- Add transitional words and phrases to show the relationship between ideas.

Editing. Remind students that good writers are also editors. They check their work for correct grammar, spelling, capitalization, and punctuation.

In a test-taking situation, students want to write as legibly and clearly as possible from the start. However, if they have extra time, they might consider rewriting their essay neatly before submitting it.

Graphic Organizers

Encourage students to use graphic organizers to

- Develop a plan for their essay.

- Focus their attention on key elements of the assignment or prompt.

- Organize and represent their thoughts in a clear and manageable way.

- Retrieve information quickly and effectively.

- Improve comprehension skills.

- Facilitate the recall of information and data.

The most effective way to guide students in using graphic organizers is to employ a think-aloud strategy. By explaining the process aloud as you create the organizer, you are modeling when and why each one is used.

Different graphic organizers can be used depending on the assignment. In social studies, students are often required to write persuasive and expository essays in which they compare and contrast two events, people, or documents; explain cause-and-effect relationships; or defend an opinion. Some practical graphic organizers for social studies writing are

- Venn diagrams to compare and contrast.

- Idea webs and flowcharts to show cause-and-effect relationships.

- Multiple-column charts and outlines to state and defend an opinion.

Writing Assessment

Students' ability to demonstrate knowledge of social studies content through writing is a key component of standardized assessment. How clearly and concisely they respond to writing prompts and essay questions is critical to their overall success on these tests.

How can I help my students manage their time effectively during an essay test?

To help students prepare for writing essays, encourage them to be aware of how much time they have to devote to this portion of an exam. For example, if they have one hour to answer an essay, they might spend one-fourth of the time (15 minutes) for prewriting, half the time (30 minutes) for writing their essay, and the remaining one-fourth (15 minutes) for revising and editing. If they finish early, they might consider rewriting the final draft more neatly.

How can I assess my students' writing?

This Annotated Teacher's Edition contains a scoring rubric that helps to evaluate your students' writing on the tests. This rubric can also be used to score any of the essay prompts in the practices found in each chapter.

This scoring rubric is similar to the ones used on standardized tests. Writing is assessed in the following areas:

- How thoroughly students address all aspects of the task (or prompt) by accurately analyzing and interpreting a series of primary sources

- How effectively students incorporate relevant outside information

- How well students support an idea with accurate facts and relevant examples and details

- How organized and fully developed an essay response is

Sample Document-Based Question Essays

▼ Test 1, Student Edition page 99

Sample Essay

There have been many great leaders throughout ancient and modern history. These leaders dedicated themselves to solving the problems of their nations in different ways. Yet, all great leaders possess similar qualities that allow them to achieve their goals and make a positive impact on society.

First, a great leader should be knowledgeable. Hammurabi of ancient Babylon and Augustus Caesar of Rome used their intelligence to find ways to reorganize their nations in a fair and effective manner. Second, a great leader should have vision. Simón Bolívar and Theodore Roosevelt were able to see beyond bad situations and find positive solutions. Determination is another quality needed to be a great leader. Despite years of discrimination, Mohandas Gandhi of India and Nelson Mandela of South Africa helped to bring about change in their countries.

These great leaders were able to make a positive impact on society because they were knowledgeable, hard working, positive minded, and determined. They were able to use their own strengths to make their nations strong.

▼ Test 2, Student Edition page 107

Sample Essay

People have migrated, or moved around, throughout the history of the world. They have sought either a temporary or permanent change of residence. People migrate for economic, social, and political reasons.

Early peoples migrated for economic reasons. Able to cross land bridges to get from one region to the next, they moved around seeking food and other sources to make clothing and build shelters. In the early second century B.C., people in Asia also migrated for economic reasons. They traveled along the Silk Road. This road offered people the opportunity to trade and learn about other parts of the world.

The Vikings migrated for social reasons. They were living in an overpopulated region. Therefore, they conducted raids in coastal areas in Europe, robbing and killing the inhabitants.

In 1992, many Somalians left their country for political reasons. Because of the civil war in Somalia, many people were starving and lost their homes.

Generic Scoring Rubric: Essay

Score of 5

- Addresses all aspects of the task by accurately analyzing and interpreting at least four documents
- Incorporates information from the documents in the body of the essay
- Incorporates relevant outside information
- Richly supports the theme or problem with relevant facts, examples, and details

- Develops essay well, consistently demonstrating a logical and clear plan of organization
- Introduces the theme or problem by establishing a framework that is beyond a simple restatement of the task or historical context and concludes with a summation of the theme or problem

Score of 4

- Addresses all aspects of the task by accurately analyzing and interpreting at least four documents
- Incorporates information from the documents in the body of the essay
- Incorporates relevant outside information
- Includes relevant facts, examples, and details, but discussion may be more descriptive than analytical

- Develops essay well, demonstrating a logical and clear plan of organization
- Introduces the theme or problem by establishing a framework that is beyond a simple restatement of the task or historical context and concludes with a summation of the theme or problem

Score of 3

- Addresses most aspects of the task or addresses all aspects of the task in a limited way, using some of the documents
- Incorporates some information from the documents in the body of the essay
- Incorporates limited or no relevant outside information

- Includes some facts, examples, and details, but discussion is more descriptive than analytical
- Develops essay satisfactorily, demonstrating a general plan of organization
- Introduces the theme or problem by repeating the task or historical context and concludes by simply repeating the theme or problem

Score of 2

- Attempts to address some aspects of the task, making limited use of the documents
- Presents no relevant outside information
- Includes few facts, examples, and details; discussion restates contents of the documents

- Organizes essay poorly, lacking focus
- Fails to introduce or summarize the theme or problem

Score of 1

- Shows limited understanding of the task with vague, unclear references to the documents
- Presents no relevant outside information
- Includes little or no accurate or relevant facts, details, or examples

- Attempts to complete the task but demonstrates a major weakness in organization
- Fails to introduce or summarize the theme or problem

Score of 0

- Fails to address the task, page is illegible or blank

Generic Scoring Rubric: Constructed Response

Score of 2

- Interprets the primary source correctly
- Demonstrates a clear understanding of the question
- Provides a complete and well-supported answer to the question

Score of 1

- Interprets the primary source with limited success
- Demonstrates a vague or incomplete understanding of the question
- Provides some correct information in response

Score of 0

- Does not understand the primary source
- Fails to address the question
- Does not provide a response

Generic Scoring Rubric: Activity

Name_____ Date_____

Activity Title_____

Directions Use the following criteria and rating chart to evaluate a completed student project. Give the student a score for each criterion. Add the points for a total score.

	Score of 4	Score of 3	Score of 2	Score of 1
Topic	Choice of topic, purpose, and audience is highly effective and appropriate.	Choice of topic, purpose, and audience work together successfully in most instances.	Topic chosen is not always appropriate for the audience.	Choice of topic does not relate to purpose and audience.
Organization	Shows excellent understanding of the goal of the assignment; evidence of careful planning; presents material in a logical sequence that can be followed.	Shows solid understanding of the goal of the assignment; evidence of good planning; presents material in some logical fashion.	Shows some understanding of the goal of the assignment; some evidence of planning; not consistently well-organized.	Shows little or no understanding of the goal of the assignment; poorly planned and difficult to follow.
Content knowledge	Presents facts, opinions, and conclusions accurately and clearly; point of view is convincing and informed.	Some facts are not fully supported; point of view is convincing and informed most of the time.	Presents some facts and opinions, some of which are not fully supported or accurate; point of view is not convincing or well informed.	Offers few facts, opinions, or conclusions; no point of view expressed on the topic.
Presentation	High level of originality and creativity; all elements work together effectively; conclusion leaves audience with a memorable and positive impression.	Strong evidence of originality and creativity; most elements work together to create a positive impression; some room for improvement.	Occasional evidence of originality and effort; elements come together sporadically.	No sign of originality or effort.
Group dynamics	Group members listen to one another, consider each other's opinions and suggestions, resolve conflicts, share or divide responsibilities fairly and equitably, work to ensure successful completion and presentation of project.	Group members listen to one another and consider each other's opinions most of the time, resolve conflicts with little teacher intervention, share or divide responsibilities fairly and equitably, complete the assignment on time, present the project effectively.	Group members listen to certain members more than others, involve teacher to resolve conflicts, attempt to share or divide responsibilities, attempt to complete and present the project.	Group members argue or ignore one another, inequitably assign work across the group, fail to complete and present the project.

Total Score_____ Final Grade_____

xvi

USING PRIMARY SOURCES

Level C

with Document-Based Questions

GLOBE FEARON

Pearson Learning Group

Contents

How to Prepare for a Test

Do you ever feel nervous before taking a test? If you do, you are not alone. Many students are anxious before a test because they want to do well. This book is especially designed to help you prepare for taking tests in world history and in other subjects.

General Tips for Taking Tests

Here are some general tips to think about before taking any test.

- ◆ Know the purpose for taking the test. If you do not know, ask your teacher to explain it to you.

- ◆ Be clear about how much time you have to take the test.

- ◆ Read all of the directions carefully so you know what is expected of you.

- ◆ If you are not sure what a question means, restate it in your own words.

- ◆ Test questions do not progress from easy to difficult. Easy questions can be found throughout the test.

- ◆ Keep track of how much time you have to take each section of the test. Set realistic times for finishing all parts of the test. Pace yourself so that you do not spend too much time on one part of the test.

- ◆ It is always better to guess than to not answer a question.

- ◆ If you have time at the end of the test, check your work.

Taking a Multiple-Choice Test

You can become "testwise" by considering these helpful tips.

- ◆ Be sure to read the entire question. Identify key terms that tell you what to look for in an answer. As you read the question, try to anticipate or guess what you think the answer will be.

- ◆ Read all possible answers before choosing one. Continue reading the possible answers, even if you think you have found the correct one. You may be surprised to find that the last answer is actually the correct one.

- ◆ Choose the best answer. If you are not certain that an answer is correct, first eliminate the answers that you know are wrong. If you eliminate one or two wrong answers, you have a better chance of picking the correct one.

- ◆ Budget your time. If you are not sure about the answer to a question, move on to the next question. If you have time at the end of the test, return to the questions you did not answer.

Answer Sheets for Multiple-Choice Tests

In this book, you will circle the correct answer in a multiple-choice question. However, most standardized tests require that you record your answers on a separate answer sheet. Here are some tips to keep in mind as you use answer sheets.

◆ Make neat, full marks.

◆ Completely erase any mistakes.

◆ Mark only one answer per item. If more than one answer is marked, it will be scored as incorrect.

◆ Avoid making any extra marks on your answer sheet. An optical scanner may misread these extra marks as your answers.

◆ It is easy to lose your place when marking answers on an answer sheet. Make sure each question and answer line up. Use a sheet of paper as a guide if necessary.

Taking a Constructed-Response or Short-Answer Test

In this book, you will have many opportunities to practice writing answers to constructed-response questions. Always remember the following tips as you answer these questions.

◆ Study the primary source carefully. If it is a map, chart, graph, timeline, political cartoon, photograph, or poster, be sure to read all captions and labels. If it is a historical document, newspaper article, firsthand account, diary entry, or letter, read the text carefully. Make note of key terms.

◆ Sometimes your answer will focus directly on the primary source you have just studied or read. Other times, you may need to recall information you have learned in world history class to help you answer a question.

◆ Organize your thoughts and express yourself clearly and concisely.

◆ Write neatly.

◆ Write your answer in complete sentences.

◆ Proofread what you have written. Check for correct grammar, spelling, capitalization, and punctuation.

How to Write an Essay

What Is an Essay?

An essay is a short, written composition. It consists of a series of paragraphs that work together and support a thesis, or single main idea.

What Is the Purpose of an Essay?

Essays are useful to inform, persuade, entertain, or narrate. Most often, you will be asked to write an informative essay on a social studies test. This kind of essay presents facts and supporting details about a specific topic. Sometimes, you will be asked to write a persuasive essay, presenting an opinion you might have, that is backed up by supporting details.

Why Is Essay Writing Important?

You will be asked to write essays on standardized tests. To succeed, you will need to organize ideas, express ideas clearly, and support ideas with factual evidence. In this book, you will have many opportunities to practice and master your essay-writing skills.

What Are the Parts of an Essay?

An essay consists of the three following parts:

1. Introduction
The introduction, or beginning of your essay, introduces the thesis, or main idea. If your essay is answering a specific question, be sure to include the answer in the introduction.

2. Body
The body, or middle, of your essay includes details that support your main idea. These details include facts and examples.

3. Conclusion
In the conclusion, or ending, you will sum up what you have written and restate the main idea, using different words.

The Writing Process

To write a well-written essay, it is important to follow the five-step process listed below:

1. Managing Your Time

- ◆ Find out how much time you have to write your essay. Then, set aside time for each step of your writing process. For example, if you have one hour to complete the essay, you might want to do the following:

  - 15 minutes for prewriting

  - 30 minutes for writing

  - 15 minutes for revising and editing

2. Prewriting

- ◆ The prewriting, or planning stage, is when you decide on a topic. If you are given an essay question or topic, it may help you understand what it means by rewriting the question in your own words.

- ◆ Use a graphic organizer to plan your essay. For example, you may use a Venn diagram to compare and contrast information. An idea web or flowchart will help show cause-and-effect relationships.

3. Writing

- ◆ Organize your ideas into complete sentences. Put related ideas into paragraphs.

- ◆ Write freely without editing and revising your work. You will have time for that later.

- ◆ Leave extra space between lines so you can edit later.

4. Revising

- ◆ Read your essay to make sure it answers the assignment.

- ◆ Be sure that each paragraph contains a main idea and supporting details.

- ◆ Improve your draft by deleting any information that does not relate to the topic. Add transitional words or phrases to show how ideas relate to each other.

5. Editing

- ◆ Check your work for correct grammar, spelling, capitalization, and punctuation.

- ◆ If you have time, you may want to rewrite your essay as neatly and legibly as possible.

Historical Documents

Model Lesson: The Universal Declaration of Human Rights

◆ Here's the Skill

"Everyone has the right to life, liberty, and the security of person."

Does this quotation sound familiar to you? It is very similar to a statement found in the Declaration of Independence, but it is not from that document. This quotation is from the Universal Declaration of Human Rights, a historical document written by members of the United Nations in 1948. The authors of the Universal Declaration of Human Rights were inspired by historical documents such as the Declaration of Independence.

Historical documents provide important information about the past. They are actual written records that have survived through time. Often, these documents are produced by or for the governments of nations.

In this chapter, you will be reading and analyzing five different types of historical documents. The first is a declaration, which is a formal public statement of a group's purpose or intent. The second is a code, or collection of laws. The third is a treatise, which is a book or piece of writing that deals with a particular subject. The fourth is a treaty, or a formal agreement between two or more governments or nations. The last is a speech, which is an oral presentation given in person or on radio or television.

The five historical documents you will read will give you a glimpse into what life was like during different times in history. You will learn about the formation of governments and how they functioned. You will also discover what people were thinking and feeling in particular periods in history.

◆ Here's Why

As you learn how to analyze historical documents, you will gain knowledge of how and why people of different nations held certain beliefs. These beliefs include the laws and policies of governments and how these impacted each nation's citizens in the past and citizens of our world today.

Being able to analyze historical documents will allow you to reconstruct and interpret important events from the past. Learning about the past helps you to understand how our world has changed or remained the same over time.

Read *A Snapshot From History* to learn more about the Universal Declaration of Human Rights, the document on page 10.

A Snapshot From History ■■■■■■■■■■■■■■■■

After World War II, many nations felt the need to form an organization that could maintain international security and peace. In 1945, the United Nations was established to help solve social, political, and cultural problems around the world.

Because of terrible acts that were committed during World War II, the United Nations wanted to protect the rights and freedoms of people in nations under its **jurisdiction**, or control. In 1948, members of the United Nations wrote and adopted the Universal Declaration of Human Rights. This document promotes and supports basic freedoms, called **human rights**, for people worldwide.

Today, many people around the world are concerned with protecting these rights. The Universal Declaration of Human Rights guides the actions of many countries and groups. Amnesty International is one organization that was established to fight, make public, and examine human rights abuses and violations. Many organizations and nations continue to work toward protecting the rights and freedoms described in the Universal Declaration of Human Rights.

Terms to Know

jurisdiction
an area of authority

human rights
the basic freedoms that all people should have

◆ Here's How

Here is a step-by-step strategy to help you analyze historical documents. Following is a passage from the Universal Declaration of Human Rights. This declaration was adopted by the United Nations on December 10, 1948.

From The Universal Declaration of Human Rights (1948)

> Identify the title of the document.

> Identify when it was written.

The General Assembly proclaims this Universal Declaration of Human Rights as a common standard of achievement for all peoples and all nations, to the end that every individual and every organ of society, keeping this Declaration constantly in mind, shall strive by teaching and education to promote respect for these rights and freedoms and by progressive measures, national and international, to secure their universal and effective recognition and observance, both among the people of Member States themselves and among the peoples of territories under their jurisdiction.

> Identify the purposes of the document.

Article 1
All human beings are born free and equal in dignity and rights. They are endowed with reason and conscience and should act towards one another in a spirit of brotherhood.

Article 2
Everyone is entitled to all the rights and freedoms set forth in this Declaration, without distinction of any kind, such as race, colour, sex, language, religion, political or other opinion, national or social origin, property, birth, or other status. Furthermore, no distinction shall be made on the basis of the political, jurisdictional, or international status of the country or territory to which a person belongs.

Article 3
Everyone has the right to life, liberty, and security of person....

> Find and look up any unfamiliar words.

Article 14
(1) Everyone has the right to seek and to enjoy in other countries asylum [a place that gives protection] from <u>persecution</u>. (2) This right may not be invoked [asked for] in the case of prosecutions genuinely arising from non-political crimes or from acts contrary to the purposes and principles of the United Nations.

> Identify the main idea of each section.

Now, review the plan on the next page. It will help you analyze this passage. Then, use the plan as you study the other historical documents in this chapter.

1. Read and Study

- ◆ Identify the document. Determine when it was written and who wrote it.

- ◆ Identify the parts of the document. Each part introduces a new idea.

- ◆ Identify the purpose and audience of the document.

2. Ask Yourself Questions

Answer the following questions about the document on page 10.

1. Who wrote the document?

members of the the United Nations

2. What are the main ideas of the first paragraph?

The document was written to help promote respect for human rights

and freedoms.

3. What are the main ideas of Article 2?

Everyone has the right to the freedoms included in the document regardless

of race, sex, religious or political beliefs, or origin.

4. What are the main ideas of Article 14?

People are allowed to leave their country of origin if they are being

treated badly and go to another country for protection.

5. According to the document, why was it written?

It was written to make a strong statement that people's rights need to be

protected, no matter who they are or where they live.

3. Put It All Together

Write an essay on a separate sheet of paper. Use specific details and information from the document in your essay.

What was the UN's purpose in writing this declaration? Explain at least three basic rights set forth in the document.

Put It All Together
See page xiv of this book for a scoring rubric.

The document's purpose is to educate people around the world and promote ways to ensure that all people have the same rights and freedoms. Three basic rights are the right to life, liberty, and security of person.

Practice 1

Analyzing Historical Documents

The Justinian Code

Here is a passage taken from the code of laws written during the reign of the Byzantine emperor Justinian. Read *A Snapshot From History* to learn more about the document.

From The Justinian Code (529–565)

Justice is the constant and perpetual desire to give to each one that to which he is entitled. Jurisprudence is the . . . comprehension of what is just and what is unjust. . . . The following are the precepts [principles] of the Law: to live honestly, not to injure another, and to give each one that which belongs to him.

There are two branches of this study, namely, public and private. Public Law is that which concerns the administration of the Roman government; Private Law relates to the interests of the individuals. Thus Private Law is said to be threefold in its nature, for it is composed of precepts of Natural Law, of those of the Law of Nations, and of those of the Civil Law.

Natural Law is that which nature taught to animals, for this law is not peculiar to the human race, but applies to all creatures which originate in the air, or the earth, and in the sea. . . . All peoples that are governed by laws and customs make use of . . . the Civil Law. . . . But the law which natural reason has established among all mankind and which is equally observed among all peoples, is called the Law of Nations, as being that which all nations make use of.

A Snapshot From History

The most famous of all leaders of the Byzantine Empire was Justinian, who took the throne in 527. He built up the empire, erecting churches, forts, and **aqueducts**. He also strengthened military forces to protect against invasion and tried to end disputes within the Christian Church.

Justinian is most remembered for organizing, updating, and clarifying the laws of the empire. He assigned this task to scholars in 528. Six years later, a large collection of laws and legal opinions, known as the Justinian **Code,** was produced. Its books contained the laws of the Roman Empire, a collection of important legal opinions, a textbook that taught students about the law, and new laws issued by Justinian between 534 and 565. After Justinian died in 565, his code lived on and continued to serve the empire for hundreds of years.

Terms to Know

aqueduct
a system of pipes and bridges used to carry water long distances

code
a set of laws

Primary-Source Questions

Use your knowledge of social studies and your world history textbook to help you analyze this document.

Multiple Choice

Read each item carefully. Circle the number of the correct answer.

1. **Which emperor called for a code of laws to be written?**

   1 Byzantine

   ② Justinian

   3 Napoleon

   4 No emperor called for a code of laws.

2. **Which of the following is not one of the principles of the Law?**

   1 to live honestly

   2 to give each one that which belongs to him

   ③ to live together peacefully

   4 not to injure another

3. **Public Law concerns**

   ① the administration of the Roman government.

   2 the administration of the Italian government.

   3 no administration.

   4 interests of individuals.

4. **The code was established to**

   1 overthrow the Byzantine emperor.

   2 eliminate Roman law.

   3 answer the people's questions.

   ④ organize, clarify, and explain Roman law.

Essay

Write an essay on a separate sheet of paper. Use specific details and information from the document in your essay.

According to the Justinian Code, why do we need laws in society?

Essay

See page xiv of this book for a scoring rubric.

Laws help to regulate what goes on in a society. According to Justinian, they help people to live honestly, not injure each other, and keep what belongs to them. Without laws, people and nations would not be responsible or held accountable for their actions.

Essay Writing Tip

◆ Before you write, take the time to plan your essay. Decide on a main idea and create an outline.

Practice 2

Analyzing Historical Documents

Two Treatises of Government

Here is a passage from John Locke's *Two Treatises of Government*.
Read *A Snapshot From History* to learn more about the document.

From John Locke,
Two Treatises of Government (1690)

If man in the state of nature be so free, . . . if he be absolute lord of his own person and possessions, . . . why will he part with his freedom? Why will he . . . subject himself to the dominion [a self-governing nation] and controul of any other power? To which it is obvious to answer, . . . the enjoyment of the property he has in this state is very unsafe, very unsecure. This makes him willing to quit a condition, which, however free, is full of fears and continual dangers: and it is not without reason, that he seeks out, and is willing to join in society with others, who are already united, or have a mind to unite, for the mutual preservation of their lives, liberties, and estates, which I call by the general name, property.

   The great and chief end, therefore, of men's uniting into commonwealths, [nations] and putting themselves under government, is the preservation of their property.

A Snapshot From History

During the **Enlightenment**, English philosophers, such as John Locke, wrote about religion, reason, nature, the physical world, and human nature. In his *Two Treatises of Government,* Locke explains his beliefs concerning politics and the rights of individuals in society.

Locke believed that people possess certain basic rights, including the right to life, liberty, and property. He felt that rulers should govern fairly and only with the people's consent. Locke explained that a government existed to protect people's basic rights. He argued that a government should be like a **contract** between the ruler and the ruled. If the people give up some individual rights to a ruler, they should receive fair rule in return. A ruler who denies basic rights to the people should be removed from power.

Many of Locke's beliefs are reflected in two important American political documents, the Declaration of Independence and the Constitution of the United States of America.

Terms to Know

Enlightenment
the eighteenth-century movement when thinkers believed they could logically explain human nature

contract
a legally binding agreement

Primary-Source Questions

Use your knowledge of social studies and your world history textbook to help you analyze this document.

Constructed Response

Read each question carefully. Write your answer on the lines provided.

Test Tip

◆ Before you read a passage, scan the questions. Then, as you read, mark phrases that will help you answer the questions.

1. **Who wrote this treatise and when was it written?**

   The English philosopher John Locke wrote it in 1690.

2. **According to the law of nature, what right does man have?**

   Man has the right to be free.

3. **What question did Locke pose in this document?**

   Why would man give up absolute freedom and allow himself to be governed?

4. **According to Locke, is man safe or unsafe in his natural state? Explain.**

   In his natural state, man is unsafe. He is free but constantly in danger.

Essay

Write an essay on a separate sheet of paper. Use specific details and information from the document in your essay.

How does John Locke explain people's willingness to unite together to form nations?

Essay

See page xiv of this book for a scoring rubric.

Locke believed that people are naturally free, but in this state of freedom, they are unprotected. People are willing to unite as nations in order to protect themselves and their property.

Practice 3
Analyzing Historical Documents

The Treaty of Nanjing

Here is a passage from The Treaty of Nanjing. Read *A Snapshot From History* to learn more about the document.

From The Treaty of Nanjing (1842)

Whereas a Treaty between Us and Our Good Brother The Emperor of China, was concluded and signed in the English and Chinese Languages, on board Our Ship the *Cornwallis*, at [Nanjing]. . . .There shall henceforward be Peace and Friendship between Her Majesty the Queen of the United Kingdom of Great Britain . . . and His Majesty the Emperor of China, and between their respective Subjects, who shall enjoy full security and protection within the Dominions of the other. . . .

British Subjects . . . shall be allowed to reside, for the purpose of carrying on their Mercantile [trade] pursuits, without molestation or restraint at the Cities and Towns of Canton, Amoy, Foochowfu, Ningpo, and Shanghai. . . .

His Majesty the Emperor of China cedes [hands over] to Her Majesty the Queen of Great Britain, etc., the Island of Hong Kong, to be possessed in perpetuity [forever] by her Britannic Majesty. . . .

The Government of China . . . [shall] permit them [British merchants] to carry on their mercantile transactions with whatever persons they please; and His Imperial Majesty further agrees to pay to the British Government the sum of Three Millions of Dollars, on account of debts due to British Subjects.

A Snapshot From History ▪▪▪▪▪▪▪▪▪▪▪▪▪▪▪▪▪▪▪

In the 1700s, there was a growing demand in Great Britain and other European nations for Chinese **exports**, such as tea, silk, and pottery. To help pay for the Chinese products they purchased, British merchants sold a drug called opium to the Chinese people.

The Chinese government tried to stop the sale of opium because many Chinese people became addicted to it. However, Great Britain continued to trade opium illegally. In 1839, the Chinese government seized all opium warehouses owned by British merchants in China. Later that year, war broke out between China and Great Britain. The Opium War, as it was known, lasted from 1839 to 1842. The **Treaty** of Nanjing ended the war.

Terms to Know

export
goods sent out of a country to be sold in another country

treaty
a formal agreement between two or more nations

Primary-Source Questions

Use your knowledge of social studies and your world history textbook to help you analyze this document.

Multiple Choice

Read each item carefully. Circle the number of the correct answer.

1. **The Treaty of Nanjing was between**

   1 Great Britain and Japan.

   ② Great Britain and China.

   3 the United States and China.

   4 the United States and Great Britain.

2. **The treaty was signed on board the ship**

   1 *Majesty.*

   2 *Cornwall.*

   ③ *Cornwallis.*

   4 *Britannica.*

3. **According to the treaty, China had to do all of the following except**

   1 pay outstanding debts.

   2 surrender the island of Hong Kong.

   3 allow British merchants to conduct business.

   ④ close all ports.

4. **The treaty**

   ① favored Great Britain.

   2 favored China.

   3 favored neither nation.

   4 was ignored by China.

Essay

Write an essay on a separate sheet of paper. Use specific details and information from the document in your essay.

What did Great Britain gain from The Treaty of Nanjing?

> ### Test Tip
>
> ◆ Once you eliminate a choice, cross it out. Then, focus on the choices that remain.

Essay

See page xiv of this book for a scoring rubric.

The British gained a great deal from the treaty. British merchants were allowed to live in certain Chinese towns. Hong Kong was given over to Great Britain, and the Chinese government paid Great Britain $3 million to cover debts owed to British subjects.

Practice 4

Analyzing Historical Documents

Speech by Nicaraguan President Violeta Chamorro

Here is a passage from a speech by Violeta Chamorro. Read *A Snapshot From History* to learn more about the speech.

From Violeta Chamorro, Democracy Award Acceptance Speech (1991)

Democracy is what unites a city in Europe and a city in Central America, despite historic differences. In my homeland, the advent [arrival] of democracy did not occur through violence or force. It took place solely through free elections. For the first time in the history of the twentieth century, the result of the vote ended a totalitarian dictatorship and the two civil war opponents agreed on peace—not because of the victory of one group, but because of the conviction of both. . . . For me, patience is the key for promoting peace—I don't believe in using force for any reason, and while I try to maintain due respect for other's viewpoints, I am always trying to convince them of mine. . . . I don't believe that violence or force can win anyone over. Those who govern a country have to be the first democrats so that democracy can exist. Government leaders and the way they govern provide the best examples of democracy for people.

A Snapshot From History

Violeta Chamorro and her husband, a newspaper editor, published articles that criticized Anastasio Somoza, the **dictator** of Nicaragua. Because of his work, Chamorro's husband was imprisoned and later assassinated. The public's outrage over his death sparked a revolution that led to the defeat of the Somoza government in 1979. At first, Chamorro supported the new government. However, she soon began to disagree with how it ran the country.

Chamorro became a candidate in Nicaragua's next free presidential election. She spoke out against **censorship** and large military spending, addressed unemployment issues, and promoted democracy. In 1990, Chamorro won the election and became Central America's first woman president. The next year, she was honored by the National Endowment for Democracy, a nonprofit group created to strengthen democracy around the world, and was given their annual Democracy Award.

Terms to Know

dictator
a ruler of a government who has absolute power

censorship
the policy of banning objectionable materials, such as books or newspapers

Primary-Source Questions

Use your knowledge of social studies and your world history textbook to help you analyze this document.

Constructed Response

Read each question carefully. Write your answer on the lines provided.

1. **According to Chamorro, what unites a city in Europe and a city in Central America?**

   democracy

2. **How was a democratic government put in place in Nicaragua?**

   A democratic government was put in place through a free election.

3. **Explain what Chamorro believes is the key for promoting peace.**

   Patience, not violence or force, is the key for promoting peace.

4. **What is one role of a democratic leader?**

   to provide an example of democracy for the people

Essay

Write an essay on a separate sheet of paper. Use specific details and information from the document in your essay.

Explain how, according to Chamorro, patience and democracy might work together.

Essay

See page xiv of this book for a scoring rubric.

A patient leader or government listens to the views of the people, encourages free thinking and expression, and opposes the use of force to gain support. Chamorro stated that in Nicaragua, democracy came about through free elections— a much slower and more patient process than a violent revolution.

Activity

In this chapter, you read passages from historical documents that focus on the struggle for all people to gain human rights and basic personal freedoms. Using newspaper and magazine clippings, create a bulletin-board display that illustrates current events related to this struggle.

Political Cartoons

Model Lesson: Napoleon Bonaparte and William Pitt

◆ Here's the Skill

Do you enjoy looking at and reading the comics section of the newspaper? If so, you would probably enjoy political cartoons. Political cartoons are usually found in magazines and in the editorial section of a newspaper. These illustrations provide a commentary, or remarks, about government, current events, people, or culture. Political cartoons emphasize or provide a humorous perspective on a particular point of view or belief.

Cartoonists who draw political cartoons often create drawings called caricatures that exaggerate a person's qualities or physical features and emphasize an opinion. For example, if a leader of a country is thought to be a bully, the cartoonist might draw that leader larger than life, looming over the country's citizens. Through the caricature, the cartoonist tries to persuade the reader to consider his or her point of view.

Cartoonists also use symbols, or pictures that stand for something else, in political cartoons. For example, if the purpose of a cartoon is to comment on an environmental issue, the cartoon might feature someone wearing a gas mask. The mask would suggest a polluted environment.

In addition to symbols, many political cartoonists include labels and captions to help the reader understand the cartoon's meaning. Reading these labels and captions provides insight into the cartoonist's point of view.

Because political cartoons can be drawn and published in a short amount of time, they usually reflect issues that are current. A well-drawn political cartoon can influence public opinion about an event, issue, or person in power.

◆ Here's Why

Political cartoons offer a reader different perspectives on an issue. By learning how to analyze political cartoons, you will discover and better understand different points of view and issues affecting governments and society that were important during a particular time in history.

Read *A Snapshot From History* to learn more about the political cartoon on page 22.

A Snapshot From History ▪▪▪▪▪▪▪▪▪▪▪▪▪▪▪▪▪▪

Napoleon Bonaparte was born in 1769 in Corsica, an island in the Mediterranean Sea. He spent his early years training at military colleges and academies in France before becoming a general in the French Revolution in 1793. At this time, he sharpened his military skills, learning how to rapidly move his armies and strike quickly. This strategy helped him succeed in many land battles. In 1799, Napoleon became first **consul** and dictator of France, and a few years later, crowned himself emperor.

By 1800, France controlled much of the European continent. Great Britain, however, opposed France. British leaders were concerned that France was planning an invasion. William Pitt, prime minister of Great Britain from 1783 to 1801 and 1804 to 1806, spent large sums of money to expand the British military. As France prepared to invade Great Britain, the two countries' navies fought near Spain. Great Britain won this naval battle at Trafalgar, ending France's hopes for invasion.

By 1809, most of the countries in Europe were dominated by France. Great Britain, however, controlled the seas and most of the trade in and out of European ports.

Term to Know

consul
a high-ranking government official

◆ Here's How

Here is a step-by-step strategy to help you analyze political cartoons that you may find on tests or see in newspapers or magazines. The following political cartoon shows Napoleon Bonaparte of France and William Pitt of Great Britain.

- Identify the main characters.

- Find each symbol and determine what it stands for.

- Tell what the main characters are doing.

▲ Pitt (left) and Napoleon (right) divide the world between France and Great Britain in 1805.

- Read the caption, or brief description, of the illustration.

Now, review the plan on the next page. It will help you analyze this political cartoon. Then, use the plan as you study the other political cartoons in this chapter.

1. Read and Study

◆ Pay attention to every detail of the cartoon. Find each symbol and determine what it stands for.

◆ Identify the main characters and what they are doing.

◆ Read any words or labels found in the cartoon. They often express the cartoonist's opinion of the issue.

◆ Read the caption, or description, of the picture. It helps place the cartoon in a historical period.

◆ Keep a list of any words you do not know. Then, look up the definitions in a dictionary.

2. Ask Yourself Questions

Answer the following questions about the political cartoon on page 22.

1. Who are the main characters? What are they doing?

Napoleon, emperor of France, and William Pitt, prime minister of Great

Britain; they are carving up the world.

2. Find two symbols in the cartoon. What does each symbol stand for?

The object being carved stands for the world. The swords stand for the war

between both nations.

3. What information can you learn from the caption?

the names of the people in the cartoon and the year of the event

4. What is the main idea of the cartoon?

France and Great Britain had the power to divide the world between

themselves.

3. Put It All Together

Write an essay on a separate sheet of paper. Use specific details and information from the cartoon in your essay.

Describe the political cartoonist's opinion of Napoleon and Pitt.

Put It All Together
See page xiv of this book for a scoring rubric.

The cartoonist does not have a high opinion of either Napoleon or Pitt. He exaggerates their features in an unflattering way. For example, Pitt is very thin and Napoleon is very short. They do not look like men who should have as much power as they do.

Practice 1
Analyzing Political Cartoons

Peter the Great

Here is a political cartoon of Peter the Great during his reign as emperor of Russia. Read *A Snapshot From History* to learn more about the cartoon.

▲ This Russian cartoon shows Peter the Great cutting off the beard of a noble.

A Snapshot From History ▪▪▪▪▪▪▪▪▪▪▪▪▪▪▪▪▪

In 1696, Peter the Great became **czar** of Russia. He ruled Russia as an **absolute monarch** until his death in 1725. During his rule, Peter the Great spent time in European countries, learning about western society. Later he ordered reforms that led to the rapid modernization of Russia. These reforms forced Russians to give up some of their traditions. One example of his reforms was a high tax on wearing beards. This tax was created to force people to adopt western hairstyles. Another example was the introduction of the European calendar. During Peter's reign, wealthy Russians began to travel and study in Europe. By the nineteenth century, French almost replaced Russian as the primary language of the noble class.

Terms to Know

czar
the Russian word for *Caesar,* which means "emperor"

absolute monarch
a ruler who is not limited by laws or a constitution

Primary-Source Questions

Use your knowledge of social studies and your world history textbook to help you analyze this political cartoon.

Multiple Choice

Read each item carefully. Circle the number of the correct answer.

1. **Who is cutting the beard in the cartoon?**

   1 a Russian noble

   2 Ivan V

   ③ Peter the Great

   4 a European noble

2. **What does the beard symbolize?**

   1 European traditions

   2 Asian influences

   3 new Russian customs

   ④ Russian traditions

3. **What does the cutting of the beard symbolize?**

   1 the westernization of Europe

   ② the westernization of Russian society

   3 western Europe trying to modernize Russia

   4 Peter the Great's attempt to keep Russian traditions alive

4. **Which symbol is NOT used in the cartoon?**

   1 scissors

   ② European calendar

   3 hat

   4 beard

Essay

Write an essay on a separate sheet of paper. Use specific details and information from the political cartoon in your essay.

Describe how the political cartoon reflects what is happening in Russia in the early 1700s.

Test Tip

◆ Read the entire question and all possible answers before making a choice.

Essay

See page xiv of this book for a scoring rubric.

Peter the Great was responsible for the westernization and modernization of Russia in the early 1700s. The cartoon shows him cutting off the beard of a Russian noble. The cutting of beards was symbolic of becoming more like western Europeans. The clothes worn by Peter and the noble are also very different. Peter's clothes are probably more like those worn by western Europeans.

Practice 2
Analyzing Political Cartoons

China's Changing Economy

Here is a political cartoon about China's changing economy in the 1980s. Read *A Snapshot From History* to learn more about the cartoon.

▲ This cartoon uses the symbol of an important historical landmark in China, the Great Wall. The caption reads, "We have a new landmark since we started our experiments with capitalism.... It's called the Great Mall of China."

A Snapshot From History

In the late 1970s, many changes were taking place in China. China's leader, Deng Xiaoping, believed in the economic system of **socialism** in which all property and wealth was owned by the community. However, he was willing to use **capitalism** as a way to strengthen and expand China's economy. Deng Xiaoping implemented a plan to improve agriculture, industry, national defense, and science and technology. One of his goals was to make China an economic world power by the twenty-first century.

Deng called his blend of socialism and capitalism a **socialist market economy**. In the late 1970s and early 1980s, some Chinese cities were opened to foreign trade and investment. Economic reform occurred in the areas of banking, taxes, trade, and investments. There were also reforms in education. Because of economic and education reforms, the Chinese people were exposed to foreign influences and ideas.

Terms to Know

socialism

an economic system in which the means of production are collectively owned or owned by the government

capitalism

an economic system based on the investment of money in businesses for profit

socialist market economy

an economic system that blends features of socialism with features of capitalism

Primary-Source Questions

Use your knowledge of social studies and your world history textbook to help you analyze this political cartoon.

Constructed Response

Read each question carefully. Write your answer on the lines provided.

1. **What historical landmark is pictured in the cartoon?**

   the Great Wall of China

2. **Who do you think is conducting the tour, and who are the people taking the tour?**

   A Chinese man living during the time of Deng Xiaoping is conducting the

   tour, and foreign tourists, possibly Americans, are taking the tour.

3. **What is the mall a symbol of?**

   The mall stands for capitalism because a mall consists of different kinds of

   businesses making money for profit.

4. **Why do you think the cartoonist used this landmark and turned it into a mall?**

   The Great Wall of China was built to defend against invaders. By turning it into

   a mall, the wall no longer keeps people out but invites them in to spend money.

Essay

Write an essay on a separate sheet of paper. Use specific details and information from the political cartoon in your essay.

How do you think Deng Xiaoping would have viewed this political cartoon?

Essay

See page xiv of this book for a scoring rubric.

Deng Xiaoping might have thought the cartoonist did not take the economic reforms in China seriously. He felt that his reforms were a necessary step to make China stronger and improve the lives of his people. By turning an important historical landmark into a mall, the cartoonist is making it seem as if the reforms were less important than they were.

Essay Writing Tip

◆ Put related ideas into paragraphs. Check that each paragraph contains a main idea and supporting details.

Practice 3
Analyzing Political Cartoons

Before and After September 11, 2001

Here is a political cartoon showing how the world was affected by terrorist attacks in the United States on September 11, 2001. Read *A Snapshot From History* to learn more about the cartoon.

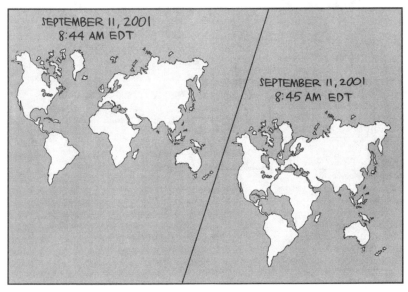

SEPTEMBER 11, 2001
8:44 AM EDT

SEPTEMBER 11, 2001
8:45 AM EDT

▲ This political cartoon shows the world before and after terrorists attacked the United States on September 11, 2001.

A Snapshot From History ■■■■■■■■■■■■■■■■■

On the morning of September 11, 2001, members of the terrorist group al Qaeda attacked the United States. They flew planes into the Twin Towers of the World Trade Center in New York City and the Pentagon in Washington, D.C., killing thousands of people. A fourth plane crashed in western Pennsylvania. Al Qaeda had previously been linked to terrorist attacks on Americans and others around the world. Many consider the attacks on September 11 to be the worst attacks on the United States since the bombing of Pearl Harbor in 1941. There was a feeling among Americans that life had forever changed. One change was that Americans realized that the United States was at risk for acts of violence known as **terrorism**.

Immediately after September 11, there were many changes in the United States. The U.S. economy took a sharp downturn and Americans lived in fear of more attacks. The government shifted its focus to combating terrorism and keeping Americans safe. Nations around the world offered their assistance and came together in the fight against terrorism.

Term to Know

terrorism
the use of threats, force, or acts of violence to frighten governments or people to change their policies

Primary-Source Questions

Use your knowledge of social studies and your world history textbook to help you analyze this political cartoon.

Constructed Response

Read each question carefully. Write your answer on the lines provided.

1. **When did terrorists attack the United States?**

   September 11, 2001

2. **What is pictured in this cartoon?**

   A map of the world is pictured at two different times (before and after the

   attacks on September 11).

3. **What is different about the second map?**

   All of the continents have moved so that they are close to one another.

4. **What is the main idea of this cartoon?**

   After being attacked by terrorists, the United States became "closer" to the

   problems and dangers facing the rest of the world. The United States, like

   other countries, was now at risk to experience the devastating effects of

   terrorism.

Essay

Write an essay on a separate sheet of paper. Use specific details and information from the political cartoon in your essay.

On September 11, 2001, U.S. President George W. Bush said, "America and our friends and allies join with all those who want peace and security in the world and we stand together to win the war against terrorism." Does the political cartoon on page 28 support President Bush's statement? Explain.

Essay

See page xiv of this book for a scoring rubric.

The political cartoon does support President Bush's statement. In the cartoon all of the nations of the world are brought closer together, which shows that the world was united in many ways after the terrorist attacks.

Practice 4
Analyzing Political Cartoons

Saddam Hussein

Here is a political cartoon about former Iraqi dictator, Saddam Hussein. Read *A Snapshot From History* to learn more about the cartoon.

▲ Saddam Hussein greets weapons inspectors from the United Nations.

A Snapshot From History

In 1990, Iraqi forces, led by Saddam Hussein, invaded Iraq's neighbor, Kuwait, to gain control of Kuwait's oil fields. The United Nations (UN) authorized the use of force to end the invasion, and on January 16, 1991, the Persian Gulf War began. This war ended six weeks later when Iraqi forces were removed from Kuwait.

After the war ended, Iraq was not allowed to produce certain weapons. Iraq was also required to cooperate with UN weapons inspectors who would check to make sure no weapons were being made. However, over the next decade, Hussein refused to cooperate fully with inspectors, often barring them from entering Iraq.

On March 17, 2003, after months of **diplomacy**, U.S. President George W. Bush ordered Hussein to leave Iraq or face war. Hussein refused, and a few days later, Iraq was attacked by U.S. and allied forces. The attack was called Operation Iraqi Freedom.

Term to Know

diplomacy
negotiations or discussions between countries

Primary-Source Questions

Use your knowledge of social studies and your world history textbook to help you analyze this political cartoon.

Multiple Choice

Read each item carefully. Circle the number of the correct answer.

1. **Who is pictured in the cartoon?**

   1 President George W. Bush

   2 President George H. W. Bush

   ③ Saddam Hussein

   4 a UN weapons inspector

2. **Who is being welcomed back to Iraq?**

   1 U.S. government officials

   ② UN weapons inspectors

   3 Saddam Hussein

   4 leaders from around the world

3. **Which of the following symbols is NOT used in this cartoon?**

   1 a carpet that is rolled out

   2 a welcome banner

   ③ weapons

   4 an "I love UN" button

4. **What is the main idea of this cartoon?**

   1 Hussein is fully cooperating with inspectors.

   2 Hussein is angry that he must cooperate with inspectors.

   ③ Hussein is pretending to cooperate with inspectors while secretly "covering up" weapons.

   4 Hussein is stepping down as Iraq's leader.

Essay

Write an essay on a separate sheet of paper. Use specific details and information from the political cartoon in your essay.

What is the cartoonist's message? How do the symbols used in the cartoon support this message?

Test Tip

◆ Read the cartoon's caption. It may contain the answer to a question.

Essay

See page xiv of this book for a scoring rubric.

The cartoonist does not trust Saddam Hussein. The cartoonist thinks that the Iraqi leader is trying to hide weapons. Hussein appears friendly, but he is standing on a carpet that hides the symbol of danger.

Activity

Study political cartoons in newspapers, on the Internet, or in magazines. Brainstorm a political issue that is of interest to you. Then, draw a cartoon that reflects your point of view. Be sure to include a title, a caption, and any important words or phrases that support your opinion.

Firsthand Accounts

Model Lesson: The Burning of Rome

◆ Here's the Skill

Have you ever interviewed someone to feature in an article for your school newspaper? Have you ever watched a person being questioned in a courtroom? If you wrote down what you heard and saw in either of these situations, it would be an example of a firsthand, or eyewitness, account. Firsthand accounts are historical documents that record one person's account of an event, description of a person, or memory of a period in his or her life. Firsthand accounts provide insights into people and events from the past.

The same event can be viewed by two people very differently. As a result, their accounts can be very different. For example, if an army soldier gave an interview about a battle that took place, his or her firsthand account might be very different from that of a soldier in the opposing army. A football player's account of a game might contain many details missing from an account by a fan who watched the game on television. These differences occur because each person's account is influenced by his or her opinion, or point of view, and his or her role in the event. Therefore, when reading and analyzing firsthand accounts, it is important to try to distinguish facts from opinions and to understand the point of view and role of the person giving the account.

Examples of firsthand accounts include information written in letters or e-mails. Autobiographies, journals, diaries, and typewritten accounts of live radio or television broadcasts, called transcripts, are also considered firsthand accounts.

◆ Here's Why

Think of a time in history and a particular event that interests you. If you could read a firsthand account from someone who had witnessed this event, you might better understand why it happened. You might learn details about the event that are not found in your world history textbook. All the firsthand accounts in this chapter are important sources for information about the past. Reading them will add to your understanding of important events and people in history.

Read *A Snapshot From History* to learn more about the firsthand account of the burning of Rome in A.D. 64 on page 34.

A Snapshot From History

On July 18, 64, a fire broke out in the city of Rome. The fire spread quickly through the city, destroying everything in its path. The fire lasted for six days and seven nights. When it was finally put out, about 70 percent of the city had been burned.

Although his involvement in the fire was never proven, many Romans believed that Nero, emperor of Rome, was responsible for starting the fire. Nero was not in Rome during the fire, and he denied all charges that he was responsible. As rumors persisted, Nero tried to avoid suspicion by blaming others.

Before the fire, Nero had lost popularity with the Roman people. After the fire, in an attempt to improve his reputation, Nero rebuilt Rome in the Greek style of architecture. He began construction on a grand palace called the Golden House, which, when finished, would fill one-third of Rome's space. Soon, marble and stone structures filled the city and Rome became a more magnificent place.

◆ Here's How

Here is a step-by-step strategy to help you analyze firsthand accounts. Following is a passage from a firsthand account by Tacitus, a historian who was in Rome during the large, destructive fire that began on the evening of July 18, 64. The account was written around the year 116.

From Tacitus, The Annals (ca. 116)

Now started the most terrible and destructive fire which Rome had ever experienced. It began in the Circus [a large amphitheater in Rome], where it adjoins [is next to] the Palatine and Caelian hills. Breaking out in shops selling inflammable [capable of catching fire] goods, and fanned by the wind, the conflagration [destructive fire] instantly grew and swept the whole length of the Circus. There were no walled mansions or temples, or any other obstructions which could arrest [stop] it. First, the fire swept violently over the level spaces. Then it climbed the hills—but returned to ravage the lower ground again.... The ancient city's narrow winding streets and irregular blocks encouraged its progress.

Terrified, shrieking women, helpless old and young, people intent on their own safety, people unselfishly supporting invalids or waiting for them, fugitives and lingerers alike—all heightened the confusion. When people looked back, menacing flames sprang up before them.... When they escaped to a neighbouring quarter, the fire followed.... Some who had lost everything—even their food for the day—could have escaped, but preferred to die. So did others, who had failed to rescue their loved ones. Nobody dared fight the flames. Attempts to do so were prevented by menacing gangs. Torches, too, were openly thrown in, by men crying that they acted under orders. Perhaps they had received orders. Or they may just have wanted to plunder [rob] unhampered.

- Identify the title and the author.

- Identify the main idea of the account.

- Identify, if possible, the setting—time and place—of the account.

- Look up any words that are unfamiliar.

- If possible, determine the author's role in the event and his or her opinion of the event.

Now, review the plan on the next page. It will help you analyze this firsthand account. Then, use the plan as you study the other firsthand accounts in this chapter.

1. Read and Study

- ◆ Identify the title and author of the account.

- ◆ Use the title and details from the account to identify the main idea.

- ◆ Determine the setting—time and place—of the account.

- ◆ Identify the position, job, or role that the author held.

- ◆ Identify the author's opinions, views, or beliefs about the event.

- ◆ Keep a list of any words you do not know. Then, look up the definitions in a dictionary.

2. Ask Yourself Questions

Answer the following questions about the firsthand account on page 34.

1. Who wrote the account?

Tacitus, a historian

2. What are the setting and date of the account?

Rome, July 18, 64

3. What is the main idea of the account?

A fire destroyed most of Rome and killed many people.

4. Identify the role of the author in the event. What is his opinion of the event?

Tacitus was present and observing what was going on during the fire. He said it was the most destructive fire that Rome had ever experienced. He saw menacing gangs stopping people from putting out the fires. He also saw people throwing lighted torches, shouting that they were acting under orders. But he was not sure whether they had received orders or just wanted to rob the city.

3. Put It All Together

Write an essay on a separate sheet of paper. Use specific details and information from the firsthand account in your essay.

Explain how this firsthand account provides information about how people responded to the fire in Rome.

Put It All Together

See page xiv of this book for a scoring rubric.

Tacitus used adjectives such as *terrified*, *shrieking*, *helpless*, and *unselfish* in his description of the event. These words provide the reader with a more in-depth view of what happened. The author also observed that people just gave up. He assumed they did so because they lost everything, or they could not rescue their loved ones.

Practice 1

Analyzing Firsthand Accounts

The Geographer, al-Bakri

Here is a passage from a book written by a geographer, Abu Ubaydallah al-Bakri. It tells about King Tunka Manin who ruled the empire of Ghana in western Africa beginning in 1063. Read *A Snapshot From History* to learn more about the firsthand account.

From al-Bakri, The Book of Routes and Realms (1067–1068)

The king ... sits in audience or to hear grievances against officials in a domed pavilion around which stand ten horses covered with gold-embroidered materials. Behind the king stand ten pages holding shields and swords decorated with gold, and on his right are the sons of the vassal kings [lords] of his country wearing splendid garments and their hair plaited [braided] with gold.... When people who profess the same religion as the king approach him they fall on their knees and sprinkle dust on their heads, for this is their way of greeting him. As for the Muslims, they greet him only by clapping their hands....

The best gold found in his land comes from the town of Ghiyaru, which is eighteen days' traveling distance from the king's town over a country inhabited by tribes of the Sudan.... The nuggets found in all the mines from his country are reserved for the king, only this gold dust being left for the people.... The nuggets may weigh from an ounce to a pound. It is related that the king owns a nugget as large as a big stone.

A Snapshot From History

In 1067, Abu Ubaydallah al-Bakri lived in the city of Cordova in the land that is present-day Spain. He was a geographer who wrote detailed descriptions of life in his region. Al-Bakri is recognized for his writings about western Sudan in Africa. His writings provide important information about the early history of that part of Africa.

Al-Bakri studied the writings of those who came before him. He also gathered **oral history** and other oral statements by interviewing merchants and others who traveled frequently to Africa. Conducting these interviews helped al-Bakri obtain information about Ghana, one of the earliest, most important trading empires in western Africa.

Term to Know

oral history
the history of a people that is told by storytellers

Primary-Source Questions

Use your knowledge of social studies and your world history textbook to help you analyze this firsthand account.

Constructed Response

Read each question carefully. Write your answer on the lines provided.

1. **Who was al-Bakri writing about?**

   Al-Bakri is writing about Tunka Manin, the king of Ghana.

2. **What does the king do while sitting in his domed pavilion?**

   He sits in audience receiving guests or hears grievances against officials.

3. **Who has a different religion from the king? How do they greet him?**

   The Muslims have a different religion. They greet him only by clapping

   their hands.

4. **Describe three features of the king's pavilion.**

   The pavilion is domed, surrounded by horses, and covered in rich fabrics.

5. **Why is al-Bakri's firsthand account important?**

   It provides us with details about the government, people, and society of the

   empire of Ghana during the eleventh century.

Essay

Write an essay on a separate sheet of paper. Use specific details and information from the firsthand account in your essay.

What does this passage from al-Bakri's writings tell us about Ghanaian society?

Test Tip

◆ Write at least one full sentence as an answer to a constructed-response question. Restate part of the question in your answer.

Essay

See page xiv of this book for a scoring rubric.

Ghana was ruled by a powerful king who was well protected by pages who surrounded him holding shields and swords. The king controlled much of the empire's wealth. For example, all of the gold nuggets belonged to the king. The people of Ghana were allowed to express their grievances, and they had different ways of formally greeting the king.

Essay Writing Tip

◆ Before writing your essay, take notes as you reread the material.

Practice 2
Analyzing Firsthand Accounts

Hernán Cortés

Here is a portion of a letter written by the explorer Hernán Cortés to the king of Spain, describing the city of Tenochtitlán in present-day Mexico. Read *A Snapshot From History* to learn more about the firsthand account.

From Cortés, Letter to the King of Spain

The great city of Tenochtitlán . . . has many open squares in which markets are continuously held and the general business of buying and selling proceeds. . . . Every kind of merchandise such as may be met within every land is for sale there, whether of food and victuals [provisions], or ornaments of gold and silver, or lead, brass, copper, tin, precious stones, bones, shells, snails and feathers. . . . There are barber shops where you may have your hair washed and cut. There are other shops where you may obtain food and drink. There are street porters such as we have in Spain to carry packages. . . . There are many different sorts of fruits including cherries and plums very similar to those found in Spain. . . .

The city contains many large and fine houses. . . . All the nobles of the land owing allegiance to Moctezuma have their houses in the city. . . . Every day in all the markets and public places of the city there are a number of workmen and masters of all the manner of crafts waiting to be hired by the day.

A Snapshot From History

Hernán Cortés was born in 1485. In 1519, he set sail for the land of Mexico from Spain. After landing at different spots along the Mexican coast, he eventually traveled to the interior. In November 1519, he reached the city of Tenochtitlán, capital of the Aztec Empire. The Aztecs ruled a large empire in what is now central and southern Mexico.

Tenochtitlán was an impressive city, with ornate palaces and temples. The Aztecs had an effective system of trade, a form of writing using **hieroglyphics**, number symbols to record important events, and a calendar based on the movements of the Sun.

Moctezuma, the Aztec emperor, welcomed the **conquistador** Cortés, who then quickly established headquarters in the city and overtook Moctezuma. Within two years, Cortés conquered the Aztecs. He became ruler of a large territory that stretched from the Caribbean Sea to the Pacific Ocean.

Terms to Know

hieroglyphics
picture writing

conquistador
the Spanish term for *conqueror*, or one who gains control by winning a war

Primary-Source Questions

Use your knowledge of social studies and your world history textbook to help you analyze this firsthand account.

Multiple Choice

Read each item carefully. Circle the number of the correct answer.

1. **Hernán Cortés is most remembered for being a**

   1   farmer.

   ② conqueror.

   3   historian.

   4   governor.

2. **The Aztecs called their capital city**

   1   Spain.

   2   Mexico City.

   3   Moctezuma.

   ④ Tenochtitlán.

3. **In his letter, Cortés commented that this "great city" had**

   1   no markets for the buying and selling of goods.

   2   nobles managing the markets.

   3   markets that bought and sold only food and clothing.

   ④ many markets for the buying and selling of all kinds
       of merchandise.

4. **Cortés observed that**

   ① the Aztecs had fruits similar to those found in Spain.

   2   the Aztecs wore clothes similar to those worn in Spain.

   3   the Aztecs had many horses.

   4   there were no similarities between the Aztecs and the Spaniards.

Essay

Write an essay on a separate sheet of paper. Use specific details and information from the firsthand account in your essay.

Do you think Cortés's letter increased the desire of the Spanish king to conquer the Aztec Empire? Why or why not?

Essay

See page xiv of this book for a scoring rubric.

Cortés's descriptions of the wealth of Tenochtitlán probably made the Spanish king more interested in conquering the Aztecs. Cortés described the Aztecs as having a large, powerful, and wealthy empire. The Aztecs had many resources that the Spaniards wanted, such as valuable land for farming and precious metals like gold and silver.

Practice 3

Analyzing Firsthand Accounts

Emperor Kangxi of China

Here is a passage from the writings of Emperor Kangxi of China that expresses his views about what makes a good ruler. Read *A Snapshot From History* to learn more about the firsthand account.

From Kangxi, Reflections on Ruling

Giving life to people and killing people—those are the powers that the emperor has.... sometimes people have to be persuaded into morality by the example of an execution ... the ruler needs both clarity and care in punishing: his intent must be to punish in order to avoid the need for further punishing....

Hu Jianjing [and his] ... family terrorized their native area in Jiangsu, seizing people's lands and wives and daughters, and murdering people after falsely accusing them of being thieves. When a commoner finally managed to impeach [discredit] him, ... the Governor was slow to hear the case, and the Board of Punishment recommended that Hu be dismissed and sent into exile for three years. I ordered instead that he be executed with his family, and in his native place, so that all the local gentry might learn how I regarded such behavior....

I have been merciful where possible. For the ruler must always check carefully before executions, and leave room for the hope that men will get better if they are given time.

A Snapshot From History

Kangxi ruled China from 1661 to 1722. He is considered one of the strongest emperors of the Ch'ing **Dynasty**, which lasted for more than 250 years. Kangxi read many books on philosophy and history, participated in many scholarly discussions, and was guided by the teachings of Confucius. Confucius was a scholar and teacher who lived from 551 to 479 B.C. and believed that people should live good, moral lives and that rulers should govern kindly and wisely.

Kangxi took his daily administrative duties very seriously, reading through every report or document, even during wartime. During his reign, Kangxi added parts of Russia and Mongolia to the Chinese Empire and took control of Tibet. He opened four ports to foreign trade, which stimulated China's industrial growth, and worked to promote economic prosperity in the land.

Term to Know

dynasty
a group of rulers who all belong to the same family

Primary-Source Questions

Use your knowledge of social studies and your world history textbook to help you analyze this firsthand account.

Multiple Choice

Read each item carefully. Circle the number of the correct answer.

1. **Kangxi was the emperor of**
    1 Russia.
    2 Manchuria.
    ③ China.
    4 Japan.

2. **According to Kangxi, an emperor has the power to**
    ① give life to people and to kill people.
    2 conquer all surrounding lands.
    3 execute only peasants.
    4 rule a country for 50 years.

3. **Kangxi believed that a ruler's intent must be to punish**
    1 when he or she felt like it.
    2 only commoners.
    3 in order to become more powerful.
    ④ in order to avoid the need for more punishment.

4. **According to Kangxi, why must a ruler check carefully before executions?**
    1 A ruler must make sure other officials agree with the punishment.
    2 A ruler has a duty to follow the wishes of the people.
    ③ A ruler must leave room for the hope that men will get better if given the time.
    4 A ruler is not permitted to make mistakes.

Essay

Write an essay on a separate sheet of paper. Use specific details and information from the firsthand account in your essay.

In what ways did Kangxi try to be a good leader?

Essay

See page xiv of this book for a scoring rubric.

Kangxi took his job as emperor seriously. He was a hard-working leader, who devoted his time to becoming more knowledgeable and informed. He believed in being "merciful where possible," punishing with "clarity and care," and leaving room "for the hope that men will get better if they are given time."

Practice 4
Analyzing Firsthand Accounts

Elizabeth Bentley's Testimony

Here is a transcript of courtroom testimony given by Elizabeth Bentley, a young factory worker from Great Britain. Read *A Snapshot From History* to learn more about the firsthand account.

From Elizabeth Bentley's Testimony (1832)

What age are you? Twenty three . . .

What time did you begin to work at a factory? When I was six years old . . .

What kind of mill is it? Flax [plant material woven into thread] mill . . .

What was your business in that mill? I was a little doffer. [a young worker]

What were your hours of labor in that mill? From 5 in the morning till 9 at night, when they were thronged [busy]. . . .

What time was allowed for your meals? Forty minutes at noon. . . .

Explain what you had to do. When the frames are full, they have to stop the frames, and take the flyers off, and take the full bobbins off, and carry them to the roller; and then put empty ones on, and set the frames on again.

Does that keep you constantly on your feet? Yes, there are so many frames and they run so quick. . . .

Suppose you flagged a little, or were too late, what would they do? Strap [whip] us. . . .

Have you ever been strapped? Yes.

A Snapshot From History

Before the **Industrial Revolution** in the 1700s, people in Great Britain worked at home spinning thread and weaving cloth by hand. Because of the demand for cloth, machines were soon invented to increase production and people began to work in factories.

As a result of the growing **textile industry**, there was a great demand for cheap labor. Employers began hiring young women and children. Children were often hired as doffers, or workers who cleaned the machines.

Laborers worked extremely long hours in unsanitary and dangerous conditions. Eventually, the British government passed laws to protect laborers and limit child labor. Before passing the laws, hearings were held to collect testimony from laborers, employers, and others involved in the factory system. The testimony was then recorded in transcripts.

Terms to Know

Industrial Revolution
beginning in Great Britain in the mid-1700s, the shift from making goods by hand to using power-driven machines

textile industry
the manufacturing of cloth from wool, cotton, and other materials

Primary-Source Questions

Use your knowledge of social studies and your world history textbook to help you analyze this firsthand account.

Constructed Response

Read each question carefully. Write your answer on the lines provided.

1. **How young were some of the workers in the textile factory?**

   six years old

2. **What was Elizabeth Bentley's job as a child laborer?**

   She was a doffer, who cleaned the machines.

3. **How many hours a day did she sometimes work?**

   16 hours a day

4. **How difficult a job did she have?**

   She stood for 16 hours a day. The machinery moved so quickly that she had to

   also work quickly, which was exhausting. If she didn't work quickly enough, she

   was hit with a strap.

5. **What effect did testimony like this have on the British government?**

   The details given about the harsh life of a factory worker caused the British

   government to pass laws restricting child labor.

Essay

Write an essay on a separate sheet of paper. Use specific details and information from the document in your essay.

Compare and contrast conditions for workers in the nineteenth century and today.

Test Tip

◆ To better understand a question, restate it in your own words.

Essay

See page xiv of this book for a scoring rubric.

In the nineteenth century, children as young as six years old had to work up to 16 hours a day. They could be whipped if they were not working hard or fast enough. Today, laws prevent children from working in factories. Most adults only have to work eight hours a day. Safety rules make the machines in factories safer to use.

Activity

As a class, choose an event that happened at school or in your community. Write a firsthand account describing the event. Then, exchange your account with a classmate and compare each other's accounts.

Posters and Newspapers

Model Lesson: A Propaganda Poster

◆ Here's the Skill

Posters are announcements that can include both words and visuals. They are written and designed in a persuasive style and try to convince the reader to join a group, become involved in a cause, see a movie, vote for a candidate, buy something, or hire someone to perform a service, for example. Posters often have clever slogans or catchy phrases that help you remember them.

Posters can be exhibited on billboards, on walls in public spaces, in stores, in movie theaters, or in any place where people will see them. You might have posters in your classroom or in your bedroom.

Have you ever designed a poster for an event at your school, such as a yearbook sale or a car wash? The posters you display in your school target a specific audience—other students. Posters are usually designed and written for a particular group of people. For example, posters that advertise joining the army are designed to attract the attention of young men and women. Posters that feature houses for sale in a retirement community are targeting an older population.

Like posters, newspapers are powerful tools that can both inform and persuade the reader. Newspapers are primary sources that keep the public informed about local, state, national, and world issues. The articles contained in them are written by professional journalists who use a variety of factual sources to obtain their information. Many articles are written to present only the facts and are not meant to persuade the reader. However, other articles are written that present reactions, points of view, and opinions that might sway how a reader is thinking.

Here's Why

Why do you think it is important to learn to analyze posters and newspapers? Newspapers can keep you informed about how your favorite sports team is doing in the playoffs, who won the local mayoral race in your community, or even provide you with the five-day weather forecast as you plan what clothing to take on vacation. Posters keep you informed about the most up-to-date goods and services you may want to buy, including the latest book and movie releases. They can also inform you about clubs or groups in your community that you may want to join or candidates you might vote for.

The posters and newspapers included in this chapter are from the past. By analyzing them, you will have a better understanding of what people were thinking and doing many years ago.

Read *A Snapshot From History* to learn more about the poster on page 46.

A Snapshot From History

From 1933 to 1945, under the leadership of Adolf Hitler, the Nazi Party in Germany used **propaganda** to promote its ideas and guide the attitudes and actions of the German people. During this time, Paul Joseph Goebbels was appointed by Hitler as propaganda minister. Goebbels used the media to spread the beliefs of the Nazi Party. He organized mass meetings and parades. Propaganda messages were broadcast over the radio and turned into films. Literature and paintings were written and created to influence public opinion.

Posters were used as another propaganda tool to spread the Nazi Party's beliefs before and during World War II. They were displayed in public places and plastered on walls and buildings in towns and cities across Germany. The posters contained powerful slogans and symbols that were used to influence the reader and viewer. Many of the posters created in Germany between 1933 and 1945 used the same images and symbols. For example, the swastika, a symbol of the Nazi Party, represented Hitler's belief in the racial superiority of the German people. Adolf Hitler, known as the *Führer*, was often featured on posters during this time.

Many posters promoted the Hitler Youth, an organization created in 1926 to train and educate male youths in Nazi beliefs. When a boy turned 10 years old, he was registered. By 1935, almost 60 percent of all German boys were in this organization. At the ages of 16 and 17, members of the Hitler Youth became members of the Nazi Party and served in the armed forces.

Terms to Know

propaganda
the promotion of certain ideas to influence people's opinions

Führer
leader

◆ Here's How

Here is a step-by-step strategy to help you analyze posters and newspaper articles. The following poster promotes the Hitler Youth.

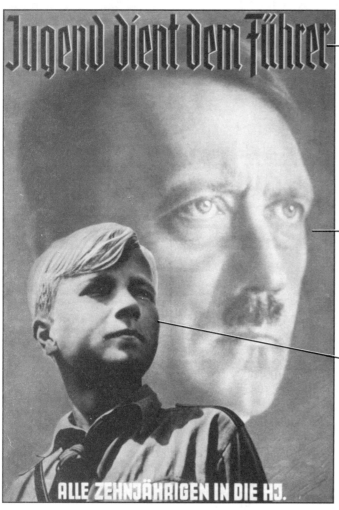

● Look at the title or slogan. If it is in a language you do not read, check the caption for a translation.

● Look at the artwork or images. What do the images show?

● Determine the audience for the poster.

▲ The text on this poster states, "Young people serve the *Führer*. All 10 year olds in the Hitler Youth."

Now, review the plan on the next page. It will help you analyze this poster. Then, use this plan as you study other posters and newspaper articles in this chapter.

● Read the caption. It provides a sense of time and place, or historical context.

1. Read and Study

◆ Pay attention to every detail in the poster. Look for answers to the questions *Who? What? When? Where?* and *Why?*

◆ Determine the main idea of the poster by reading all of the text and by studying the artwork.

◆ Read the caption to place the poster in a historical context.

◆ Keep a list of any words you do not know. Then, look up the definitions in a dictionary.

2. Ask Yourself Questions

Answer the following questions about the poster on page 46.

1. **Who is the intended audience for this poster?**

   German boys 10 years of age and older

2. **When was the poster probably created?**

   Before or during World War II

3. **Where was it created?**

   Germany

4. **What is the poster promoting?**

   It is promoting the Hitler Youth organization.

5. **Why is this organization being promoted?**

   The Nazi Party wants to encourage young boys to take part in the Hitler

   Youth and serve their country and the *Führer*.

3. Put It All Together

Write an essay on a separate sheet of paper. Use specific details and information from the poster in your essay.

Describe how the poster uses propaganda to persuade the audience to support the *Führer* and the Nazi Party.

Put It All Together
See page xiv of this book for a scoring rubric.

Although the image of Hitler is shown faintly in the background, his face takes up the entire poster, symbolizing his prominence as leader of Germany. The boy in the foreground represents all male youths in Germany more than 10 years old. By showing these two images, the poster is conveying the message that the *Führer* wants full cooperation and support from German boys.

Practice 1

Analyzing Newspaper Articles

The Tomb of King Tutankhamen

Here is a passage taken from a London *Times* newspaper article. Read *A Snapshot From History* to learn more about the article.

From The Times (London), "Tutankhamen's Inner Tomb Is Opened" (1923)

Luxor, Egypt, Feb. 16—This has been perhaps the most extraordinary day in the whole history of Egyptian excavation. Whatever any one man may have guessed or imagined of the secret of Tutankhamen's tomb, they surely could not have dreamed the truth as now revealed.

The entrance today was made into the sealed chamber of the tomb of Tutankhamen, and yet another door opened beyond that. No eyes have seen the King, but to practical certainty we know that he lies there close at hand in all his original state, undisturbed. Moreover, in addition to the great store of treasures which the tomb has already yielded, today has brought to light a new wealth of objects of artistic, historical, and even intrinsic [built-in] value.

The process of opening this doorway, bearing the royal insignia [mark] and guarded by the protective statues of the King, had taken several hours.... It finally ended in a wonderful revelation, for before the spectators was a resplendent mausoleum [tomb] of the King, a spacious and beautifully decorated chamber completely occupied by an immense shrine covered with gold inlaid with brilliant blue faience [earthenware].

A Snapshot From History

King Tutankhamen, also known today as King Tut, ruled Egypt from 1361 to 1352 B.C. as the **pharaoh**, or leader. He became pharaoh when he was only nine years old. King Tut moved the capital of Egypt back to Thebes and rebuilt temples. He died suddenly when he was about 18 years old and was buried in the Valley of the Tombs of the Kings.

Although better known than other Egyptian pharaohs, King Tut is most famous because of the discovery of his lavishly furnished tomb in 1922. The burial chamber was completely intact and untouched by robbers. Among other treasures, it contained a solid-gold coffin.

Term to Know

pharaoh
a title given to the rulers of ancient Egypt

Primary-Source Questions

Use your knowledge of social studies and your world history textbook to help you analyze this newspaper article.

Multiple Choice

Read each item carefully. Circle the number of the correct answer.

1. **Where was King Tut's tomb found?**

   1 England

   2 New York

   ③ Egypt

   4 Spain

2. **Excavation is the process of**

   1 burying a treasure.

   ② digging something out.

   3 honoring a king.

   4 carrying precious goods.

3. **What was NOT found in King Tut's tomb?**

   1 artistic and historical treasures

   2 protective statues of the king

   3 closed doors

   ④ tools left behind from other excavators

4. **Why was finding King Tut's tomb an important discovery?**

   ① Historic truths were revealed.

   2 King Tut was not found inside.

   3 It was learned that robbers had stolen many treasures.

   4 No new information was revealed about King Tut.

Essay

Write an essay on a separate sheet of paper. Use specific details and information from the newspaper article in your essay.

If you were excavating King Tut's tomb, what information would you hope to learn through analyzing the treasures?

Essay

See page xiv of this book for a scoring rubric.

Learning about what life was like in Egypt during King Tut's reign would be important information to uncover. For example, what were the roles of men and women? What kinds of jobs did they do? What kind of clothing did they wear? What were their daily activities? What was the prominent style of art during the time? What were important Egyptian beliefs? Students might hope to learn about King Tut's responsibilities during his reign, his siblings, and children. They would also want to learn how he was viewed by others, if he had enemies, and if he was revered as king.

Essay Writing Tip

◆ Before writing, organize your thoughts in a clear way. Use a graphic organizer such as a Venn diagram or an idea web to plan your essay.

Practice 2
Analyzing Posters

Labor Union Poster

Here is a poster that was created in the 1940s to promote American labor unions. Read *A Snapshot From History* to learn more about the poster.

for all these rights
we've just begun to fight

THE RIGHT TO EARN ENOUGH
TO PROVIDE ADEQUATE FOOD & CLOTHING &
RECREATION

REGISTER • VOTE

▲ This poster, drawn by Ben Shahn in 1946, encourages people in labor unions to register to vote.

A Snapshot From History

Ben Shahn, a photographer and graphic artist, was born in Russia. In 1906, his family fled a czarist **regime**, and emigrated to the United States. Shahn's photographs and illustrations included portraits of ordinary life and poverty. His posters often addressed social and political issues, including **labor union** concerns.

In 1935, the National Labor Relations Act was passed in the United States. This act, also known as the Wagner Act, allowed workers to organize and not be dominated, or controlled, by their employers. It also allowed workers to choose their **bargaining agents**. Employers were required to meet with these bargaining agents in order to resolve conflicts.

Terms to Know

regime
a government

labor union
an association of workers that protects the interests of its members

bargaining agent
a person who tries to make an agreement between two parties

Primary-Source Questions

Use your knowledge of social studies and your world history textbook to help you analyze this poster.

Constructed Response

Read each question carefully. Write your answer on the lines provided.

1. Why was the poster created?

The poster was created to encourage workers to register to vote.

2. Who was the intended audience?

The intended audience included workers and members of labor unions.

3. What were some of the rights that workers fought for during this time?

Workers wanted decent wages so they could have enough money for their needs (food, clothing, and shelter) and wants (recreation). Workers also fought for education and job security.

4. How would registering to vote help workers gain these rights?

By voting, workers would have a say in the passage of laws benefiting them in their local, state, and national elections.

Essay

Write an essay on a separate sheet of paper. Use specific details and information from the poster in your essay.

Discuss how effective you think the poster is. Describe at least two symbols or techniques used by the artist in the poster.

Test Tip

◆ Read all of the questions before studying the poster. Then, focus on the parts of the poster that will help you find the answers to the questions.

Essay

See page xiv of this book for a scoring rubric.

Students might think that the poster does a good job expressing the idea that workers must fight for their rights. The man shown in the poster has his arm raised and his hand in a fist. This shows he is ready to fight for his beliefs. He is surrounded by signs that contain lists of all the rights demanded by the workers. The main message of the poster, "Register—Vote," is clearly displayed in large type at the bottom edge.

Practice 3

Analyzing Newspaper Articles

The Disappearance of Amelia Earhart

Here is a passage taken from a *New York Times* newspaper article.
Read *A Snapshot From History* to learn more about the article.

From The New York Times, "Miss Earhart Forced Down at Sea" (1937)

Honolulu, July 2—Amelia Earhart, the world's best known aviatrix [female pilot], and her navigator, Fred Noonan, were believed forced down at sea today in their $80,000 "flying laboratory" somewhere near tiny Howland Island on a daring attempt to span the South Pacific.

Apparently, headwinds had exhausted their gasoline within 100 miles of the end of a projected 2,556-mile flight from Lae, New Guinea. . . .The cutter *Itasca* set out at 8:30 P.M. [E.D.T.] to hunt the missing plane. Coast guardsmen here expressed the belief that aviation's "first lady" and her companion had overshot the minute island and come down somewhere in the vast mid-Pacific region far removed from regular shipping lanes. The cutter prepared to search the little known area.

Bound around the world on an equatorial trail of more than 27,000 miles, Miss Earhart had flown since May 21 from Oakland, Calif., in relatively leisurely stages.

A Snapshot From History

Amelia Earhart was born in Atchison, Kansas, in 1897. Against her family's wishes, Earhart learned to fly and bought her first plane in 1922. In 1928, she became the first woman passenger to fly across the Atlantic Ocean. Then in 1932, she made history once again by becoming the first woman to cross the Atlantic alone. Earhart wrote about her flying experiences in her book, *The Fun of It*. She also encouraged women to enter the field of **aviation**.

In 1937, with a navigator aboard, she set out to fly around the world in her twin-engine plane. But before she was able to complete her trip, her plane vanished in the South Pacific and was never found. For many years people have wondered what happened to Amelia Earhart. To this day, her disappearance remains a mystery.

Term to Know

aviation
the science or art of operating and navigating aircraft

Primary-Source Questions

Use your knowledge of social studies and your world history textbook to help you analyze this newspaper article.

Multiple Choice

Read each item carefully. Circle the number of the correct answer.

1. **Who is the world's best-known aviatrix?**

   1 Eleanor Roosevelt

   2 Amanda Earhart

   3 Fred Noonan

   ④ Amelia Earhart

2. **Earhart's plane was also known as a**

   1 "flying machine."

   2 "fastest in the world."

   ③ "flying laboratory."

   4 "first lady."

3. **What was the name of the ship that searched for the plane?**

   ① *Itasca*

   2 *Ilasta*

   3 *Howland*

   4 *New Guinea*

4. **Why was Earhart referred to as aviation's "first lady"?**

   1 She was the first person to fly across the Pacific.

   2 This trip around the world was her first time flying.

   3 She was married to the President of the United States.

   ④ She was the first woman to fly across the Atlantic alone.

Essay

Write an essay on a separate sheet of paper. Use specific details and information from the newspaper article in your essay.

Summarize what was known about Earhart's flight immediately after her disappearance.

Test Tip

◆ Read all of the possible answers before selecting one.

Essay

See page xiv of this book for a scoring rubric.

Earhart and her navigator were flying near Howland Island in the middle of the Pacific Ocean when their plane was lost. They had been traveling from New Guinea and had almost reached the end of the 2,556-mile flight when they probably ran out of gas.

Practice 4

Analyzing Newspaper Articles

Tiananmen Square Massacre

Here is a passage from a *New York Times* newspaper article written by Richard Bernstein. Read *A Snapshot From History* to learn more about the article.

From Bernstein, *The New York Times*, "At China's Ministry of Truth, History Is Quickly Rewritten" (1989)

Shanghai, China, June 11—The Chinese propaganda machinery has been put into full swing, seeking to transform the event [Tiananmen Square massacre] into a heroic operation that saved the country from "a counterrevolutionary plot. . . ."

The bloody massacre described in the foreign press . . . never took place, Chinese news reports say. According to the official television stations and newspapers, what actually occurred was a largely peaceful operation, vigorously supported by public opinion. . . .

An extraordinary series of broadcasts over several nights on national television illustrates the tone of the propaganda effort. For two nights, both the early and late evening news programs broadcast segments of a street interview done by ABC News in Beijing shortly after the army's assaults. A man is shown being interviewed, his voice rising with anger and his arms imitating the motion of a machine gun, as he describes a scene of terrible carnage [slaughter] committed, he says, by the army.

A caption on the bottom of the screen during the interview identifies the man as "somebody spreading rumors about the cleanup of Tiananmen Square." After the man speaks, the news announcer warns the public to beware of believing such rumors, then says that the man is wanted by the police and he appeals to the public to turn him in.

Tonight the national news showed the same man, looking haggard and terrified, in police custody, retracting in front of the cameras what he had said to ABC News.

A Snapshot From History

In early June 1989, thousands of Chinese students occupied Tiananmen Square in the heart of Beijing, protesting their lack of political freedoms and demanding **democracy**. When students refused to leave the square, armed Chinese troops and tanks rolled in and killed thousands of people. China's government claimed this protest was a **counterrevolutionary** plot.

Terms to Know

democracy
a government that gives its citizens the ruling power

counterrevolutionary
working against a government set up by a previous revolution

Primary-Source Questions

Use your knowledge of social studies and your world history textbook to help you analyze this newspaper article.

Constructed Response

Read each question carefully. Write your answer on the lines provided.

1. **Where and when did this student uprising take place?**

   Tiananmen Square, Beijing, China; June, 1989

2. **How did the Chinese government use propaganda after the massacre to hide the truth from the public?**

   The government used television broadcasts to say that there was a peaceful

   demonstration supported by public opinion. It also manipulated television

   footage of a man describing the carnage. The footage contained a caption

   stating that he spread rumors about what happened and asked the public to

   turn him in. Then, the police arrested him and forced him to retract his

   statements.

3. **Why did the Chinese government deny that a massacre took place at Tiananmen Square?**

   It did not want anyone challenging or questioning government policy. It wanted

   to be viewed as a heroic government who saved the country from a group of

   rioters. The government wanted to manipulate what information the Chinese

   people heard in the media so that it could be in total control. It wanted to

   suppress any dissent by the masses.

Essay

Write an essay on a separate sheet of paper. Use specific details and information from the newspaper article in your essay.

Some reporters write articles that contain only facts while other reporters include their opinion or point of view. Did this reporter include his own opinions in this article? How do you know?

Test Tip

◆ Look for key terms in a question. Then, scan the text for those terms to help find the answer.

Essay

See page xiv of this book for a scoring rubric.

This journalist thinks that the Chinese government is deceitful and is trying to cover up what happened in Tiananmen Square. He uses phrases such as the "Chinese propaganda machinery" to describe China, showing that he does not believe China's version of events.

Activity

In this chapter, you analyzed a poster and a newspaper article that used propaganda to influence readers. Write a newspaper article or create a poster that convinces readers of your ideas and beliefs. Add a headline to your article or captions and images to your poster.

Photographs, Art, and Artifacts

Model Lesson: Egyptian Tomb Art

◆ Here's the Skill

Words are powerful tools used to express what people think and feel. By listening to what others say or by reading what others write, we learn a great deal about people and the world around us. However, we can also learn important information about people, places, and events by studying photographs, art, and artifacts. These important primary sources provide a visual record of daily life and show what it was like to live in different societies and at different times.

Photographs first appeared in the 1800s when photography was invented. With this development, people had a new way to relate to the world around them. Photographers could capture timely events on film and show many details in a single image. Details such as facial expressions or gestures revealed significant information that could be studied and interpreted.

Art, such as paintings, mosaics, murals, and sculpture, also helps people become more knowledgeable about the world and its history. Like photographs, different kinds of art contain many details and can capture the mood, or feeling, of the time. The attitudes and opinions of artists about a particular subject or event are frequently revealed in their work.

Artifacts, such as pottery, tools, toys, household items, and other human-made objects from the past, also help people learn about cultures throughout the history of the world. A tool can provide information about how early people built their homes. Even cloth can provide clues about what kinds of plants or animals people raised.

◆ Here's Why

Studying photographs, art, and artifacts is another way of discovering and exploring world history. These primary sources visually tell a story about the past. Learning about the past helps people gain a better understanding of the world today. Viewing photographs, art, and artifacts gives people a unique opportunity to travel back to a single moment in time.

Read *A Snapshot From History* to learn more about the ancient Egyptian image found on page 58.

A Snapshot From History ▪▪▪▪▪▪▪▪▪▪▪▪▪▪▪▪▪▪

In ancient Egypt, people of all classes shared a belief in the afterlife. Death was thought to be a necessary transition to the next world, where life would continue in a similar manner. In Egypt's Old Kingdom, which existed from about 2980 B.C. to about 2475 B.C., great **pyramids** were built. These pyramids served as the resting places for Egyptian kings and queens after their deaths. Kings, called pharaohs, were looked upon as gods, who had the power to rule even after death. The tombs of these kings were grand and impressive and carefully constructed so they could survive for a long time. Smaller tombs were built for other important members of society.

Tombs contained as much information about the dead person as possible. There were statues of the great man or woman and of his or her servants, carved pictures and words, and paintings, that told stories of how the person had lived. The tombs were often decorated with reliefs, or designs projecting from a background. These reliefs showed people involved in everyday activities such as hunting and farming. Tombs were filled with many valuable treasures as well as items like food and clothing.

In 1865, the tomb of Ti was discovered. Ti had been an Egyptian official who lived around 2400 B.C. He was a hairdresser to the royal family and managed their farms. Ti's wife, who was a relative of the royal family, and his eldest son were also buried in his tomb.

Term to Know

pyramid
a large structure with a square base and triangular sides that meet in a point at the top

◆ Here's How

Here is a step-by-step strategy to help you analyze photographs, art, and artifacts. This is a portion of a relief from the tomb of Ti in Saqqara, Egypt.

● Determine the setting—time and place—by describing the image.

● Find objects in the image and determine what they were used for.

● Pay attention to every detail, such as what this Egyptian person was carrying.

● Read the caption for additional information.

▲ Ti was an Egyptian official who served during the reign of Kakai, which lasted from 2446 to 2426 B.C. This relief shows two of Ti's servants.

Now, review the plan on the next page. It will help you analyze this relief. Then, use the plan as you study the photographs, art, and artifacts in this chapter.

1. Read and Study

- ◆ Pay attention to every detail of the image.

- ◆ Consider how the details give clues about the setting, the specific event, and the lifestyle of the people represented in the image.

- ◆ Look for clues about the artist's attitude, or feelings, about the subject of the image.

2. Ask Yourself Questions

Answer the following questions about the relief on page 58.

1. **What does this image show?**

   an Egyptian relief; two Egyptian servants

2. **Where was the tomb of Ti discovered?**

   Saqqara, Egypt

3. **Who was Ti?**

   an Egyptian official who lived around 2400 B.C.

4. **Who are the people in the relief? How can you tell?**

   The people are servants of Ti's family. They are carrying food in baskets on

   their heads and animals. They are shown in profile, walking in the same

   direction in an orderly fashion.

3. Put It All Together

Write an essay on a separate sheet of paper. Use specific details and information from the relief in your essay.

What can the art found in Egyptian tombs tell us about the everyday lives of ancient Egyptians?

Essay

See page xiv of this book for a scoring rubric.

Egyptian tomb art provides clues about the everyday lives of ancient Egyptians. For instance, the relief in Ti's tomb shows two servants carrying food. The relief shows the hairstyles, dress, and jewelry of the servants. It also shows that they used baskets to carry goods on their heads. Finally, it shows the kinds of foods Egyptians ate.

Practice 1
Analyzing Photographs, Art, and Artifacts

An Ancient Greek Vase

Here is a vase from ancient Greece. Read *A Snapshot From History* to learn more about the artifact.

▲ This hydria, an ancient Greek vase, was used to carry water.

A Snapshot From History ▪▪▪▪▪▪▪▪▪▪▪▪▪▪▪▪▪

Many of the images on ancient Greek vases provide information about everyday life in Greece. In ancient Greece, vases were considered to be works of art. Used in homes, at ceremonies, and for entertainment purposes, vases were both decorative and functional. A hydria, or water jug, was used to carry water. Other vases were used for storing supplies, such as food, wine, cosmetics, jewelry, and body oil. Vases were also used as mixing bowls and drinking cups.

Primary-Source Questions

Use your knowledge of social studies and your world history textbook to help you analyze this artifact.

Multiple Choice

Read each item carefully. Circle the number of the correct answer.

1. **What was the purpose of this ancient Greek vase?**

   1 drinking cup

   2 ceremonial

   ③ to carry water

   4 to hold grains

2. **This vase was called**

   1 an amphora.

   2 a hydra.

   3 a krater.

   ④ a hydria.

3. **The scene on the vase shows**

   1 war.

   ② everyday life.

   3 a ceremony.

   4 a funeral.

4. **Which of the following is NOT shown on the vase?**

   1 a woman reading a scroll

   2 Greek clothing, furniture, and hairstyles

   ③ women preparing a meal

   4 a woman holding a box

Essay

Write an essay on a separate sheet of paper. Use specific details and information from the artifact in your essay.

What do vases tell us about the lifestyles and art of ancient Greeks?

Test Tip

◆ If two words look almost identical, check each word's spelling against what you read in the caption or in *A Snapshot From History*.

Essay

See page xiv of this book for a scoring rubric.

Vases provide information about the ideas and lifestyles of the ancient Greeks. Vases were used for both functional and decorative purposes. They were used to store food, water, wine, cosmetics, and body oil. They were also used as mixing bowls and drinking cups. Also, they were considered works of art. An effort was made to make them beautiful as well as functional.

Practice 2

Analyzing Photographs, Art, and Artifacts

American Civil War Photograph

Here is a photograph taken by Mathew Brady. Read *A Snapshot From History* to learn more about the photograph.

▲ This photograph was taken by Mathew Brady in 1864 during the American Civil War. It shows members of the Union army at Fort Brady in Virginia.

A Snapshot From History

In 1861, **civil war** broke out between the United States federal government, called the Union, and 11 southern states. Economic differences, as well as opposing views over the issue of slavery, led the southern states to **secede** from the Union. The southern, or Confederate, states fought for four years against the Union.

The photographer Mathew Brady wanted to keep a record of important events, battles, and people during the American Civil War. He hired 20 teams of photographers to help him take photographs from 1862 to 1864. Brady took photographs of significant battles. He also photographed important people during the war, including President Abraham Lincoln and General Robert E. Lee.

Terms to Know

civil war
war between groups of people from the same country

secede
to withdraw or leave

Primary-Source Questions

Use your knowledge of social studies and your world history textbook to help you analyze this photograph.

Constructed Response

Read each question carefully. Write your answer on the lines provided.

1. **Who took this photograph?**

   Mathew Brady

2. **When and where was this photograph taken?**

   1864; Fort Brady in Virginia

3. **What are the people in this photograph doing?**

   The soldiers are standing guard inside the fort, ready to fire their weapons

   (cannons) if necessary.

4. **Why are photographs like this important?**

   It is important to keep a record of Fort Brady and the soldiers who were

   stationed there during the Civil War. People can get an idea of what kinds of

   weapons were used, what soldiers looked like, and how they fought during

   the war.

Essay

Write an essay on a separate sheet of paper. Use specific details and information from the photograph in your essay.

What does this photograph tell about how wars were fought at the time of the American Civil War?

Essay

See page xiv of this book for a scoring rubric.

Wars in the nineteenth century were primarily fought by men. Soldiers' uniforms were similar to formal men's suits, and they wore hats instead of helmets. Many battles were conducted on land. To protect a fort, soldiers used cannons and probably guns and rifles. The cannons were stationary and probably could not be moved quickly. The fort's walls were built of dirt supported by logs and stones.

Practice 3

Analyzing Photographs, Art, and Artifacts

Diego Rivera Mural

Here is a portion of a mural painted by the Mexican artist, Diego Rivera. Read *A Snapshot From History* to learn more about the mural.

▲ This mural, painted in 1945, is called *The Great City of Tenochtitlán*.

A Snapshot From History

Diego Rivera was born in Guanajuato, Mexico, on December 8, 1886. He painted bold and colorful **murals**, which covered the walls of public buildings and schools around Mexico City. Rivera painted important moments and events in Mexican history. His murals show Mexican agriculture, industry, customs, and culture.

In 1945, Rivera completed a mural he called *The Great City of Tenochtitlán*. Tenochtitlán was the capital city of the Aztec Empire. During the fourteenth century, the Aztecs built this city in the center of an enormous lake. The city grew in wealth and power until Hernán Cortés and his Spanish army invaded and conquered it in 1521. Today, the ruins of Tenochtitlán can be found under present-day Mexico City.

Term to Know

mural
a picture painted directly on a wall

Primary-Source Questions

Use your knowledge of social studies and your world history textbook to help you analyze this mural.

Multiple Choice

Read each item carefully. Circle the number of the correct answer.

1. ***The Great City of Tenochtitlán* is a**

   1 photograph.

   2 sculpture.

   ③ mural.

   4 colorful drawing.

2. ***The Great City of Tenochtitlán* shows the capital city of**

   1 ancient Egypt.

   2 the Maya Empire.

   3 the Inca Empire.

   ④ the Aztec Empire.

3. **The artist, Diego Rivera, has painted**

   ① a busy marketplace.

   2 a formal ceremony.

   3 a crowded winter festival.

   4 a hospital.

4. **If you study this mural carefully, you may learn about all of the following, except**

   1 Tenochtitlán.

   2 Aztec culture and society.

   3 Diego Rivera.

   ④ a famous battle.

Essay

Write an essay on a separate sheet of paper. Use specific details and information from the mural in your essay.

What does Rivera's mural show about Aztec society? What can you learn about the artist himself from studying it?

Essay

See page xiv of this book for a scoring rubric.

This mural shows that the Aztecs had a highly developed and advanced civilization. Markets existed for the buying and selling of goods and services, and people held different occupations and positions in society. For example, there were doctors, store owners, craftspeople, and laborers. Some people are wearing jewelry and fine clothing (suggesting wealth and status), while others are not. People learn that Rivera was interested in the history of Mexico. He was familiar with Aztec society and how the people of this civilization lived and worked together.

Test Tip

◆ The word *except* is a clue that you need to find an answer that does *not* relate to the painting.

Essay Writing Tip

◆ Write as clearly and legibly as possible. If you have time, consider rewriting your essay neatly before handing it in.

Practice 4

Analyzing Photographs, Art, and Artifacts

Japanese Barbers

Here is a photograph of Japanese barbers taken between 1870 and 1880. Read *A Snapshot From History* to learn more about the photograph.

▲ The Japanese barber on the right creates a traditional hairstyle, the chonmage.

A Snapshot From History

In Japan in 1868, a political change referred to as the Meiji Restoration took place. A group of soldiers called **samurai** overthrew their commander, the **shogun**. Power was returned to the emperor for the first time in more than two centuries. The young emperor Mutsuhito, known as Meiji, ruled the land for the next 45 years.

The new Meiji government worked to modernize Japan's economy and society. Eventually, Japanese customs also changed. For many years, Japanese men had worn the traditional hairstyle that began among the samurai, called the chonmage. After a number of years in power, the Meiji government ordered men to cut their hair in a short Western style. Only rikishi, or sumo wrestlers, were permitted to wear their hair pulled up in the chonmage as long as they continued to wrestle.

Terms to Know

samurai
  a Japanese warrior

shogun
  the supreme military commander of Japan

Primary-Source Questions

Use your knowledge of social studies and your world history textbook to help you analyze this photograph.

Constructed Response

Read each question carefully. Write your answer on the lines provided.

1. **Where and when was this photograph taken?**

   Japan; between 1870 and 1880, at the beginning of the Meiji reign

2. **What is the chonmage?**

   a traditional Japanese hairstyle, originally worn by the samurai

3. **What is happening in this photograph?**

   One barber is styling the chonmage. The second barber is shaving a man's

   face. All of the men are wearing traditional Japanese clothing.

4. **What details about Japan in the late 1800s can be gathered from the photograph?**

   Men wore kimono-style clothing; barbers shaved men and fixed their hair in

   the traditional chonmage style.

Essay

Write an essay on a separate sheet of paper. Use specific details and information from the photograph in your essay.

Historians often refer to photographs to learn about how people lived in the past. How does this photograph help people learn about Japanese society in the nineteenth century?

Essay

See page xiv of this book for a scoring rubric.

Customs and traditions are important in Japan. For example, until the 1880s, men continued wearing the traditional chonmage, a style that first began with the samurai. Also, the photograph gives people a picture of what clothing people wore in Japan in the nineteenth century.

Activity

Take photographs or paint pictures that focus on a memorable event. Create an album of these images. Under each picture, write a short caption that provides more details about the event, such as what people were doing, thinking, and feeling during this special time. Share your album with classmates.

Maps

Model Lesson: Ancient India

◆ Here's the Skill

There are many kinds of maps. Some maps, such as road maps, help people get to places they have never been to before. These maps list street names, provide possible travel routes, and help people measure the distance between different places. Sometimes, road maps highlight the location of special places in a community, such as museums, amusement parks, hospitals, or schools.

There are three basic kinds of maps: physical maps, political maps, and special-purpose maps. Maps that identify important geographical features such as mountains, plains, lakes, and oceans are called physical maps. Other maps show political divisions by illustrating specific cities, states, countries, and continents. They are known as political maps. Maps that provide specific information about a certain topic are called special-purpose maps.

In your history classes, you have probably studied many maps that contain information about a particular time in history. Historical maps are a kind of special-purpose map that can focus on many topics, such as battles, trade routes, land claims, voyages of exploration, or the movement of people. In this chapter, you will study several historical maps. They will show reasons for the downfall of an early civilization in India, the spread of the religion of Islam, the routes traveled by a Chinese explorer, and some of Africa's natural resources. One map will even show you what a town looked like 400 years ago.

A great deal of information can be found in maps. A map can show us what people thought the world looked like in their time. When you look at a map, you might even be able to find out more about why the cartographer, or mapmaker, made the map.

Here's Why

Maps contain valuable information. To be able to access the information contained in a map, you will need to use the different parts of a map, such as the map key, compass rose, and scale. These tools provide a way to analyze and interpret the map's information. The information uncovered from interpreting maps enriches people's understanding of events in history.

Read *A Snapshot From History* to learn more about the map of ancient India on page 70.

A Snapshot From History

The first organized, settled communities in the world were responsible for influencing the development of later civilizations, empires, and nations. The early groups of people who lived in these settled communities had their own cities and social structures, and some invented unique forms of writing.

The Indus Valley civilization was an ancient civilization that existed from about 2500 B.C. to about 1500 B.C. in present-day Pakistan. It is the earliest known urban, or city-based, culture of the Indian **subcontinent**.

The Indus Valley civilization had several important cities. Two of the best known are Harappa and Mohenjo Daro. There were also many towns and small villages. Each city had a **citadel**, or fortress, public baths and sewers, buildings for storing grains called granaries, and administrative buildings.

The people of the Indus Valley had a uniform culture, strong economy, and central government. Some scholars believe that groups of merchants ruled the land. Due to annual floods from the surrounding rivers, the Indus Valley was a fertile region. Many different kinds of crops were grown, such as wheat, barley, vegetables, and cotton. Cotton was used to produce **textiles**, or cloth, which were possibly traded with people from other areas.

Researchers think that around 1500 B.C., Aryan peoples from the northwest invaded the Indus region. Attacks like these as well as devastating floods are thought to be possible reasons for the disappearance of the Indus Valley civilization.

Terms to Know

subcontinent
a large part of a continent that is geographically separated from the rest of the continent

citadel
a fort that commands a city

textile
cloth manufactured from wool, cotton, or other materials

◆ Here's How

Here is a step-by-step strategy to help you analyze maps. Look at the following map of ancient India.

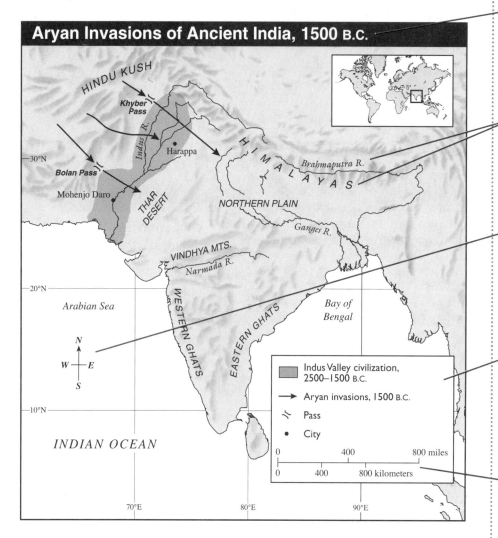

- Read the title to determine the subject, purpose, and date.

- Read all the text and labels. They indicate specific places on the map.

- Check the compass rose. It shows direction—north, south, east, and west.

- Read the map key to identify what the symbols and shades of color stand for.

- Look at the scale to see how distances on the map relate to real distances.

Now, review the plan on the next page. It will help you analyze this map. Then, use the plan as you study the other maps in this chapter.

1. Read and Study

- Read the title and map key to determine the subject, purpose, and date of the map.

- Read all the text and labels in the map.

- Pay attention to every detail such as symbols, key, scale, and shades of color.

- Use these details to interpret the map.

- Keep a list of any words you do not know. Then, look up the definitions in a dictionary.

2. Ask Yourself Questions

Answer the following questions about the map on page 70.

1. **What is the subject of the map?**

   Aryan invasions of ancient India

2. **What ancient civilization is shown on the map and from which time period?**

   the Indus Valley civilization; 2500 to 1500 B.C.

3. **What were the two large cities of this civilization?**

   Harappa and Mohenjo Daro

4. **Describe what is represented by the arrows on the map.**

   The arrows represent Aryan peoples who came from the northwest and

   invaded the Indus Valley civilization in about 1500 B.C.

3. Put It All Together

Write an essay on a separate sheet of paper. Use specific details and information from the map in your essay.

After studying the map, discuss what you have learned about the Indus Valley civilization. Include at least three facts about the civilization in your essay.

Essay

See page xiv of this book for a scoring rubric.

The Indus Valley civilization existed for about 1,000 years, from 2500 B.C. to about 1500 B.C. Harappa and Mohenjo Daro were the two main cities located in the northwest. They appear to be about 400 miles apart. These cities were built near the Indus River, which provided them with a sufficient water supply and kept the land fertile for growing crops. Some scholars believe that in 1500 B.C. Aryan peoples invaded the region from the northwest.

Practice 1

Analyzing Maps

The Spread of Islam

Here is a map showing the spread of Islam after the death of Muhammad. Read *A Snapshot From History* to learn more about the map.

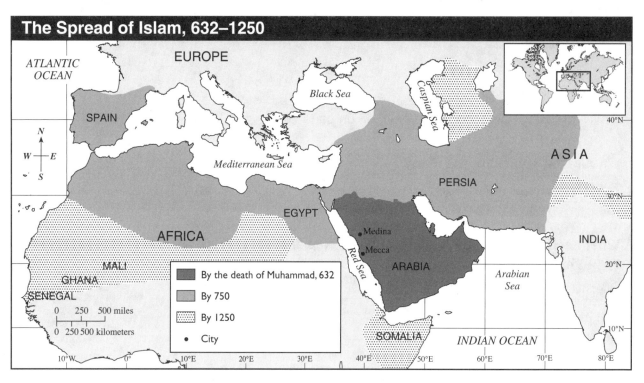

The Spread of Islam, 632–1250

By the death of Muhammad, 632
By 750
By 1250
• City

A Snapshot From History

The religion of Islam was founded by Muhammad in the seventh century. Muhammad was born in the city of Mecca, in what is now Saudi Arabia, in about 570. Years later, Muhammad spent many nights in a cave near Mecca, thinking about how life should be lived. In 610, an angel visited him in a vision and told him to spread information about God. Muhammad received numerous messages over the course of his life.

In 613, Muhammad started preaching about God, or Allah, in Mecca. Some of Muhammad's many followers collected his teachings into a book of rules and laws called the Quran. The Quran is the holy book of Islam. Some people, however, opposed Muhammad. In September 622, Muhammad and his followers left Mecca for the city of Medina, a flight called the *hijra*. In Medina they began to practice the new religion of Islam. Muhammad returned to Mecca in 630. After his death in 632, the religion spread rapidly throughout different parts of the world.

Term to Know

hijra
the flight of Muhammad and his followers from Mecca to Medina in 622

Primary-Source Questions

Use your knowledge of social studies and your world history textbook to help you analyze this map.

Multiple Choice

Read each item carefully. Circle the number of the correct answer.

1. **What does this map show?**

   1 the spread of Christianity

   (2) the spread of Islam

   3 the destruction of Islam

   4 the birth of Muhammad

2. **Muhammad died in**

   1 750.

   2 630.

   3 1250.

   (4) 632.

3. **After the death of Muhammad,**

   1 Muslims refused to conquer new lands.

   2 Muslims converted to Christianity.

   (3) more people followed the religion of Islam.

   4 few people followed the religion of Islam.

4. **According to the map, by 750, Muslims had**

   (1) controlled Persia, Spain, and North Africa.

   2 controlled only Spain.

   3 controlled Arabia.

   4 exerted no control over the Middle East.

Essay

Write an essay on a separate sheet of paper. Use specific details and information from the map in your essay.

What information does this map provide about the rise and spread of Islam?

Essay

See page xiv of this book for a scoring rubric.

By the time of his death in 632, Muhammad had many followers called Muslims, who practiced the religion of Islam in the region known as Arabia. After Muhammad's death, the Islamic religion spread. By 750, most people living in the areas of the Middle East, North Africa, and Spain practiced Islam. By 1250, Islam had spread farther into Africa and western Asia.

Practice 2

Analyzing Maps

A Map of Limerick, Ireland

Here is a map of the city of Limerick, Ireland, from the seventeenth century. Read *A Snapshot From History* to learn more about the map.

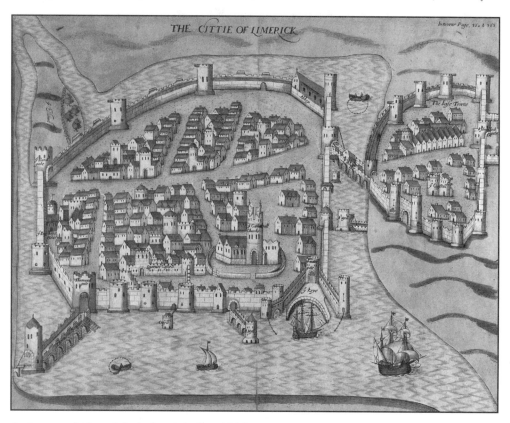

▲ A map of Limerick, Ireland, in the 1600s

A Snapshot From History ■ ■ ■ ■ ■ ■ ■ ■ ■ ■ ■ ■ ■ ■ ■ ■ ■ ■

The illustrated map on this page shows the city of Limerick as it existed in the early 1600s. Located on the west coast of Ireland and at the mouth of the Shannon River, Limerick is currently an important **port** for land and sea transportation. It occupies two banks of the river and an island called King's Island.

Limerick was an important center and stronghold, or **fortress**, for the Vikings in the early 800s. In the thirteenth century, English Town was founded on King's Island and a castle was built there. In the late seventeenth century, the castle walls were extended to include an area called Irish Town, making Limerick an even stronger fortress. Today, many fragments of the wall surrounding the city still remain.

Terms to Know

port
a city or town where ships can load and unload cargo

fortress
an enclosed place used for military defense

Primary-Source Questions

Use your knowledge of social studies and your world history textbook to help you analyze this map.

Constructed Response

Read each question carefully. Write your answer on the lines provided.

1. **What is the subject and purpose of this map?**

   the city of Limerick; the purpose of the map is to show the configuration

   of Limerick.

2. **In which century was this map drawn?**

   the seventeenth century

3. **Describe the types of transportation used during this period that are found on this map.**

   Several types of boats can be seen: large sailing ships, smaller sailing

   ships, and rowboats. Also, the city contains many roads which could be

   used for walking or horseback riding.

4. **What surrounds most of the city?**

   Water surrounds the part of the city that is located on the island. Castle walls

   surrounded the island and also the part of the city that was located on the

   river banks.

5. **Why do you think the city was enclosed in walls?**

   The walls provided protection from enemies.

Essay

Write an essay on a separate sheet of paper. Use specific details and information from the map in your essay.

Discuss the advantages and disadvantages of building a city like Limerick on an island.

Essay

See page xiv of this book for a scoring rubric.

Limerick was built on an island with strong walls surrounding it. This prevented intruders from penetrating the fortress and entering the city. In addition, its location on the river made Limerick an ideal port from which people and goods could be transported easily. A disadvantage was that people had to use boats or narrow bridges to travel to and from the city. It might have been easy to cut the city off from fresh food supplies on the mainland.

Test Tip

◆ To answer a question, you may need to think of other places you have read about. For example, what other cities are surrounded by walls?

Practice 3
Analyzing Maps

The Voyages of Zheng He

Here is a map showing the voyages of the Chinese admiral, Zheng He. Read *A Snapshot From History* to learn more about the map.

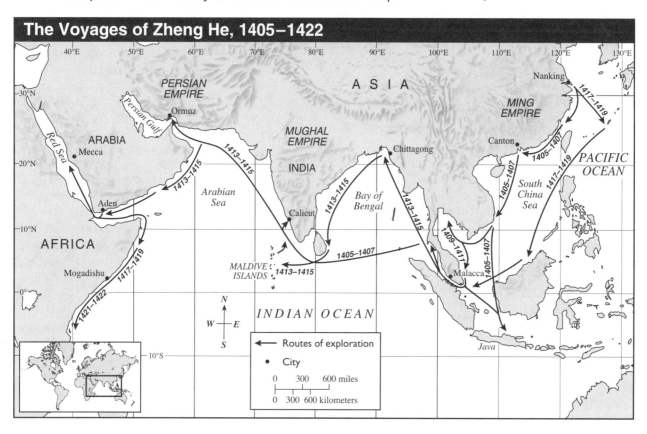

The Voyages of Zheng He, 1405–1422

A Snapshot From History

For many years, before and during the Ming Dynasty, the people of China had been building ships, traveling abroad, and expanding sea **commerce**. In 1402, Emperor Yung-lo took the throne. He wanted to demonstrate China's naval power to the rest of the world and expand China's knowledge. In 1405, he selected Zheng He to be the commander of numerous expeditions that would explore many different lands, display the splendor and power of China to the world, and expand sea commerce.

Starting in 1405, Zheng He led seven large expeditions. Admiral Zheng He and his fleet explored Southeast Asia and India, as well as Arabia and eastern Africa. These voyages brought Chinese **immigrants** into areas such as Southeast Asia.

Terms to Know

commerce
trade; the buying and selling of goods

immigrant
a person who enters a new country to live there

Primary-Source Questions

Use your knowledge of social studies and your world history textbook to help you analyze this map.

Constructed Response

Read each question carefully. Write your answer on the lines provided.

1. **Who was Zheng He?**

   He was a Chinese admiral who led expeditions to many lands starting in 1405.

2. **What do the arrows on the map represent?**

   The arrows represent exploration routes.

3. **What year was Zheng He's first voyage?**

   1405

4. **What lands did he explore?**

   He explored parts of Asia, India, Arabia, and Africa.

5. **List the bodies of water labeled on the map.**

   Pacific Ocean, South China Sea, Bay of Bengal, Indian Ocean, Arabian Sea,

   Red Sea, Persian Gulf

Essay

Write an essay on a separate sheet of paper. Use specific details and information from the map in your essay.

Why were the voyages of Zheng He significant?

Essay

See page xiv of this book for a scoring rubric.

The voyages of Zheng He allowed the Chinese to explore different lands and cultures and come into contact with people from different societies. The voyages stimulated a desire in Chinese people to live in other parts of the world, eventually leading to the increase in Chinese emigration.

Essay Writing Tip

◆ When revising your essay, add transitional words and phrases such as *however, soon, after,* and *next* to show the relationship between ideas.

Practice 4
Analyzing Maps

Africa's Natural Resources

Here is a map of some of the natural resources found in Africa. Read *A Snapshot From History* to learn more about the map.

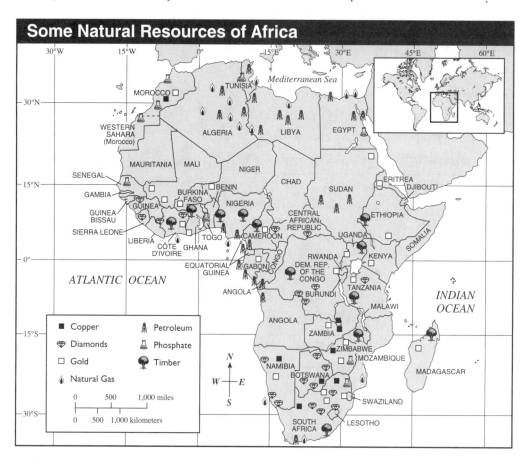

Some Natural Resources of Africa

A Snapshot From History

Africa, the world's second largest continent, is rich in **natural resources**. It contains large deposits of valuable **minerals**. Africa produces approximately 40 percent of the world's diamonds, about 50 percent of the world's gold, and is an important producer of petroleum and other minerals, including copper.

Profiting from natural resources is a significant part of Africa's economy. The abundance of natural resources in Africa is one reason why the continent was colonized by European nations beginning in the seventeenth century.

Terms to Know

natural resources
materials supplied by nature that are useful to people

minerals
substances obtained by mining

78

Primary-Source Questions

Use your knowledge of social studies and your world history textbook to help you analyze this map.

Multiple Choice

Read each item carefully. Circle the number of the correct answer.

1. **What are Madagascar's major natural resources?**

   1 petroleum and gold

   2 natural gas and gold

   3 copper and timber

   (4) gold and timber

2. **Which of these countries produces petroleum?**

   1 Mauritania

   (2) Angola

   3 Zambia

   4 Ethiopia

3. **Which section of Africa has the most diamond mines?**

   1 the northern section

   (2) the southern section

   3 the eastern section

   4 the western section

4. **Where are most of Africa's natural gas reserves?**

   (1) northern Africa

   2 Nigeria

   3 eastern Africa

   4 Sudan

Essay

Write an essay on a separate sheet of paper. Use specific details and information from the map in your essay.

Discuss Africa's natural resources. Use at least five details from the map in your essay.

Essay

See page xiv of this book for a scoring rubric.

Africa is one of the world's richest continents in natural resources. It is a leader in diamond production and produces about half of the world's gold. Other natural resources include copper, natural gas, petroleum, phosphate, and timber.

Activity

Choose a place in the world that interests you, whether historically, politically, or economically. Then, draw a map that includes information about this place. Include a title that identifies the subject, purpose, and dates. Then, share your map with the class, discussing its purpose and how the map helps convey information about this place.

Informational Graphics

Model Lesson: The World's Largest Countries

◆ Here's the Skill

Informational graphics, such as charts, graphs, and timelines, present data or other information in a visual manner. They help you to make comparisons as well as to organize and summarize information. At a glance, they present statistical data in a simple way, making information easier to understand and remember.

A chart, or table, is one way to provide visual information. Using rows and columns, charts organize categories of information. For example, a chart may list different Chinese dynasties in the first column, dates of when each dynasty existed in the second column, and contributions of each dynasty in the third column.

A circle graph contains information shown in the shape of a circle. Sometimes circle graphs are called pie graphs. The circle is divided into parts that represent different information about a single topic. For example, the topic of a circle graph may be the percentage of immigrants moving to the United States from different countries. Each part of the circle graph would represent the percentage of immigrants from a different country. By looking at the graph, you could tell which countries had the most or least immigrants.

A bar graph compares large amounts of information. For example, a bar graph might show several cities in 1800 and provide information about their populations. By looking at the heights of the bars on the graph, you could determine which cities had the largest or smallest populations.

Timelines show a series of events displayed in the time order in which those events happened. Dates are included to help organize the information. A timeline is a perfect way to organize and study historical information, such as important events during India's fight for independence from Great Britain.

◆ Here's Why

Knowing how to analyze informational graphics, such as charts, circle graphs, bar graphs, and timelines, will help you interpret and understand the information found in newspapers and magazines, as well as in books or on the Internet.

Read *A Snapshot From History* to learn more about the bar graph showing the populations of the world's largest countries on page 82.

A Snapshot From History ▪▪▪▪▪▪▪▪▪▪▪▪▪▪▪▪▪▪

Before 1750, populations in different countries around the world grew at a much slower rate than they do today. This slower growth rate was due in large part to poor health practices and unsanitary conditions. The numbers of people dying, called the **mortality rates**, for infants and children were high. Also, people did not live as long as they do today. Disease, war, and famine also contributed to the slow growth in population.

In the 1900s, especially after World War II, many countries experienced a "population explosion." This population growth was a result of improvements in nutrition, sanitation, and public health.

The world population reached 1 billion in the early 1800s. The second billion was reached in less than 100 years. The third billion took less than 50 years after that. Additional billions have been reached in time spans of 12 years each. Now, the world's population is more than 6 billion. The drop in death rates is the primary reason for this tremendous growth spurt.

Scientists who study statistics about human populations, known as **demographers**, help people understand trends occurring around the world. Demographers predict, or project, that India, with a population of about 1 billion in 2002, will increase its population to approximately 1.6 billion in 2050. For **developing countries**, population increases such as this will make it more difficult to provide adequate healthcare and educational services, jobs, and food supplies.

Terms to Know

mortality rates
death rates

demographer
a social scientist who studies population trends

developing country
a country in which industrialization is still taking place

Here is a step-by-step strategy to help you analyze informational graphics. Below is a bar graph that shows 2002 populations and population projections for the world's largest countries.

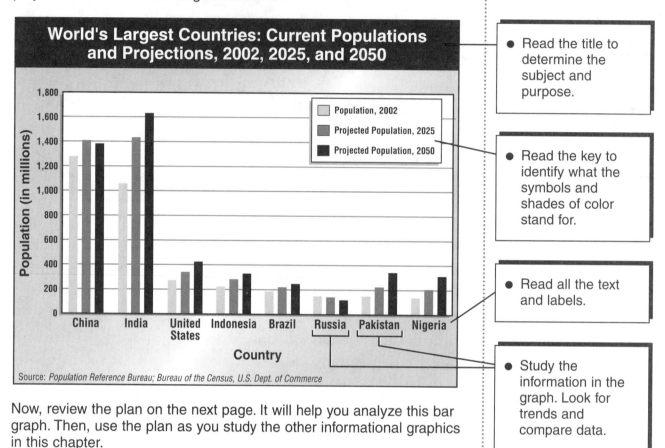

World's Largest Countries: Current Populations and Projections, 2002, 2025, and 2050

- Read the title to determine the subject and purpose.

- Read the key to identify what the symbols and shades of color stand for.

- Read all the text and labels.

- Study the information in the graph. Look for trends and compare data.

Now, review the plan on the next page. It will help you analyze this bar graph. Then, use the plan as you study the other informational graphics in this chapter.

1. Read and Study

◆ Identify the type of informational graphic shown.

◆ Read the title to determine the subject, purpose, and years of the graphic.

◆ Read all the text and numbers in the graphic.

◆ Pay attention to every detail such as symbols, keys, labels, and shades of colors used. Use these details to interpret the data, or information provided.

◆ Keep a list of words you do not know. Then, look up the definitions in a dictionary.

2. Ask Yourself Questions

Answer the following questions about the bar graph on page 82.

1. **What is the subject and purpose of this bar graph? What are the dates shown in this bar graph?**

    The subject is world populations. The purpose is to compare current

    populations and projections for the world's largest countries. The bar graph

    compares populations and projections for 2002, 2025, and 2050.

2. **Which country's population is predicted to decline in 2025 and 2050?**

    Russia

3. **Which country's population is projected to increase the most between 2002 and 2050?**

    India

4. **What was the least populated country in 2002? The most populated?**

    Nigeria; China

3. Put It All Together

Write an essay on a separate sheet of paper. Use specific details and information from the bar graph in your essay.

Describe two population trends illustrated by the bar graph.

Put It All Together

See page xiv of this book for a scoring rubric.

One trend is the rapid increase in the populations of some countries, such as India. Estimates predict that its population will climb to more than 1.6 billion in 2050. A second trend is the decrease in population in countries such as China and Russia.

Practice 1

Analyzing Informational Graphics

The Kingdoms of West Africa

Here is a chart containing facts about three kingdoms of West Africa.
Read *A Snapshot From History* to learn more about the chart.

Kingdoms of West Africa		
Ghana (ca. 500 – ca. 1200)	**Mali (ca. 1200 – ca. 1550)**	**Songhai (ca. 1335 –1591)**
• Controls gold trade across West Africa.	• Conquers the kingdom of Ghana.	• Grows into the largest West African state.
• Trades gold with the Berbers for salt.	• Mansa Musa becomes a great emperor.	• Controls important trade routes.
• Huge armies conquer nearby lands, gaining tribute and soldiers for the king.	• Controls gold trade routes.	• The emperor sets up a Muslim dynasty.
• Provides protection to conquered lands in exchange for tribute.	• Timbuktu and Gao become great trading cities and centers of learning.	• Has a strict social system and participates in the slave trade.
• The Berbers bring Islam to Ghana although the kings do not convert.	• Develops a strong government with new laws, a tax system, and a dedication to education.	• Captures Gao and Timbuktu; gains control of the trading empire.
• Kings are tolerant of Islamic religion and have Islamic advisors.	• New mosques and universities are built to develop Islamic culture.	
• People live as farmers and traders, mine gold, and weave cloth.	• Mali is larger and far richer than Ghana.	

A Snapshot From History ■■■■■■■■■■■■■■■■■■■

The kingdom of Ghana, in Africa, existed from about the sixth
century to the thirteenth century. It grew in wealth and power from
its involvement in the valuable gold and salt trades. It also received
wealth from other nations in the form of **tribute**. Eventually, war
weakened Ghana's trading empire and it lost power. It became part
of the Mali Empire.

Mali's greatest emperor, Mansa Musa, expanded Mali by invading
and gaining more lands. He effectively controlled the gold trade and
built up the cities of Timbuktu and Gao. Mali began to lose its power
and influence in the 1500s.

Songhai flourished in the fourteenth and fifteenth centuries,
becoming a significant trading state. The Songhai people profited
greatly from the gold trade. However, after numerous attacks at the
end of the sixteenth century, the kingdom collapsed.

Term to Know

tribute

payment given by
one nation to another
more powerful nation;
may be paid in
exchange for
protection

Primary-Source Questions

Use your knowledge of social studies and your world history textbook to help you analyze this chart.

Multiple Choice

Read each item carefully. Circle the number of the correct answer.

1. **What does this chart show?**

   1 ancient kingdoms around the world

   2 the trading routes of West Africa

   ③ the kingdoms of West Africa

   4 the kingdoms of North Africa

2. **According to the chart, Mali**

   1 captured Gao and Timbuktu.

   2 provided protection to conquered lands in exchange for tribute.

   ③ had a government dedicated to education.

   4 had a Muslim dynasty.

3. **Which kingdom grew into the largest West African state?**

   1 Ghana

   2 Mali

   ③ Songhai

   4 East Africa

4. **According to the chart, Ghana controlled**

   1 all markets in southern Africa.

   ② trade in gold.

   3 trade in cloth.

   4 many other empires.

Essay

Write an essay on a separate sheet of paper. Use specific details and information from the chart in your essay.

Compare and contrast the kingdoms of West Africa.

Test Tip

◆ You might be asked to turn the information found in a chart into a timeline. To do this, list events with dates in the order in which they occurred.

Essay

See page xiv of this book for a scoring rubric.

Ghana, Mali, and Songhai were three powerful kingdoms of West Africa. They grew into wealthy trading empires. Songhai was the largest of the kingdoms, and it participated in the slave trade. Mali had two cities that were famous as centers for learning. Ghana was the earliest kingdom.

Practice 2

Analyzing Informational Graphics

The Destinations of Enslaved Africans

Here is a circle graph that illustrates the destinations of enslaved Africans. Read *A Snapshot From History* to learn more about the circle graph.

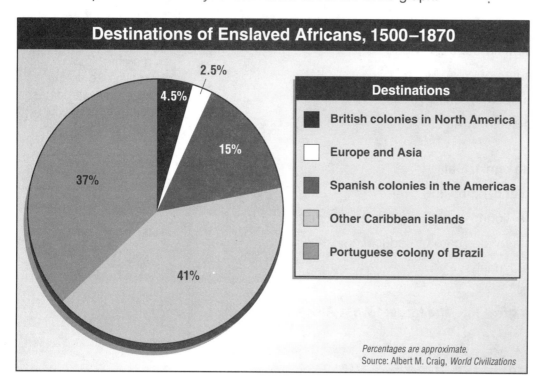

Destinations of Enslaved Africans, 1500–1870

2.5%
4.5%
15%
37%
41%

Destinations

■ British colonies in North America

□ Europe and Asia

■ Spanish colonies in the Americas

□ Other Caribbean islands

■ Portuguese colony of Brazil

Percentages are approximate.
Source: Albert M. Craig, *World Civilizations*

A Snapshot From History

Beginning in the sixteenth century, transatlantic slave trading, sometimes called **triangular trade** because of its connections to three continents, grew. Africans were captured by other Africans or by Europeans and taken to the western coast of Africa. There, they were sold to European merchants. Next, enslaved Africans were shipped across the Atlantic Ocean to North America or South America in a journey called the **Middle Passage**.

Because of harsh treatment and unsanitary conditions, from 10 to more than 20 percent of enslaved Africans died on the ships. The survivors were sold at auctions. The merchants then used the profits to buy goods that were sent to Europe. The enslaved Africans were put to work on sugar, coffee, tobacco, and cotton plantations, either as field workers or as house servants. They were also sent to work in gold and silver mines.

Terms to Know

triangular trade
a trading system involving a three-way exchange of goods and people in Europe, Africa, and the Americas

Middle Passage
the second leg of the triangular trade routes in which slaves were shipped across the Atlantic Ocean

Primary-Source Questions

Use your knowledge of social studies and your world history textbook to help you analyze this circle graph.

Constructed Response

Read each question carefully. Write your answer on the lines provided.

1. **What percentage of enslaved Africans were sent to British colonies in North America between 1500 and 1870?**

   4.5 percent

2. **What percentage of enslaved Africans were sent to Spanish colonies in the Americas between 1500 and 1870?**

   15 percent

3. **Can you tell from this graph what percentage of enslaved Africans were sent to the United States? Why or why not?**

   No, the graph only shows that 4.5 percent of enslaved Africans were sent to

   British colonies in the Americas. Some of those colonies eventually became the

   United States. Also, parts of the Spanish colonies became the United States.

4. **Can you tell from this graph what percentage of enslaved Africans were sent to all of North America? Why or why not?**

   No, the percentage of enslaved Africans sent to all of North America is not

   listed. Only the percentage of enslaved Africans sent to the British colonies

   in North America is known (4.5 percent).

Essay

Write an essay on a separate sheet of paper. Use specific details and information from the circle graph in your essay.

Describe how and where the slave trade was conducted between 1500 and 1870.

© Pearson Education, Inc. Copying strictly prohibited.

Essay

See page xiv of this book for a scoring rubric.

Africans were captured by other Africans or Europeans and then sold to European merchants. They then traveled across the Atlantic Ocean to destinations such as the Caribbean islands, Brazil, and Spanish colonies in the Americas. These were the top three destinations for enslaved Africans between 1500 and 1870.

Test Tip

◆ Sometimes a circle graph will not give you all the data or information you need. You may have to draw conclusions based on the data in the graph and what you already know.

Essay Writing Tip

◆ Use key social studies terms in your essay as often as possible.

Practice 3

Analyzing Informational Graphics

The Struggle for Independence

Here is a timeline showing when some Latin American countries gained independence during the early nineteenth century. Read *A Snapshot From History* to learn more about the timeline.

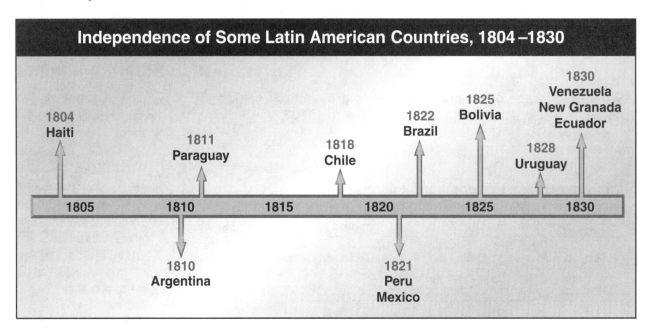

Independence of Some Latin American Countries, 1804–1830

1804 Haiti
1811 Paraguay
1818 Chile
1822 Brazil
1825 Bolivia
1828 Uruguay
1830 Venezuela New Granada Ecuador

1805   1810   1815   1820   1825   1830

1810 Argentina
1821 Peru Mexico

A Snapshot From History

Today, Latin America includes Mexico, Central America, South America, and some islands in the Caribbean Sea. In the first half of the nineteenth century, a number of Latin American **colonies** fought for and gained their independence from European nations including Spain and France, after 300 years of colonial rule. Tensions in Latin America had been growing for years, as more and more people became unhappy with European rule.

The first colony to declare its independence was Haiti, in 1804. Many independence movements were directed by Simón Bolívar, a military and political leader. José de San Martín also fought to liberate many southern South American colonies.

Those colonists fighting for independence kept fighting despite many defeats in battle. By 1830, all colonies in Latin America that had been controlled by European nations had achieved their independence except for Puerto Rico and Cuba.

Term to Know

colony
a settlement in a distant land that is governed by another country

Primary-Source Questions

Use your knowledge of social studies and your world history textbook to help you analyze this timeline.

Multiple Choice

Read each item carefully. Circle the number of the correct answer.

1. This timeline shows when

   1 Spain gained control of certain colonies.

   ② some Latin American colonies gained their independence.

   3 Cuba gained its independence.

   4 Latin American colonies battled with England.

2. According to the timeline, Haiti

   ① gained its independence in 1804.

   2 lost its independence in 1804.

   3 gained its independence after Argentina.

   4 never gained its independence.

3. What happened in 1821?

   1 Bolivia was the last country to gain its freedom.

   2 Peru surrendered to Spanish forces.

   3 Peru and Chile gained their independence.

   ④ Peru and Mexico became independent.

4. Between 1805 and 1815,

   1 Haiti gained its independence.

   2 Paraguay and Chile became independent countries.

   ③ Paraguay and Argentina became independent countries.

   4 Paraguay and Argentina surrendered to Spain.

Essay

Write an essay on a separate sheet of paper. Use specific details and information from the timeline in your essay.

What does the timeline show about Latin America in the first half of the nineteenth century?

Essay

See page xiv of this book for a scoring rubric.

In the first half of the nineteenth century, numerous Latin American colonies began fighting for their independence, beginning with Haiti in 1804. Other colonies joined the independence movement. By 1830, many colonies, including Argentina, Paraguay, Chile, Peru, Mexico, and Brazil were liberated, ending years of colonial rule.

Practice 4

Analyzing Informational Graphics

German Ships in the Americas

Here is a portion of a chart created before the United States entered World War II. It lists German ships in port in South America. Read *A Snapshot From History* to learn more about the chart.

GERMAN MERCHANT VESSELS IN THE AMERICAS

November 14, 1939.

German Merchant Vessles in Port

Country & Port	No.	Names	Type	Gross Tons
Argentina	3			
Bahia Blanca (Ingeniero)	1	Uesukuma	Pass-cargo	7834
Buenos Aires	2	Anatolia	Cargo	2446
		Nienburg	Pass-cargo	4318
Brazil	16			
Bahia	3	Antonio Delfino	Pass-cargo	13589
		Bahia	Cargo	4117
		Maoelo	Cargo	3235
Para	2	Norderney	Cargo	3667
		Königsberg	Cargo	6466
Pernambuco	3	São Paulo	Cargo	4977
		Uruguay	Cargo	5846
		Wolfsburg	Cargo	6201
Rio de Janeiro	5	Bahia Blanca	Cargo	8558
		Bollwerk	Cargo	4173
		La Coruna	Pass-cargo	7414
		Minden	Pass-cargo	4165
		Santos	Pass-cargo	5943
Rio Grande do Sul	2	Montevideo	Cargo	6075
		Rio Grande	Cargo	6062
Santos	1	Babitonga	Pass-cargo	4422

A Snapshot From History

In September 1939, World War II began in Europe. The United States, under President Franklin D. Roosevelt, hoped to avoid war. On November 14, 1939, in an effort to gather information about the war, U.S. Secretary of State Sumner Welles sent a letter to President Roosevelt. It contained a chart listing German merchant **vessels** in and around ports in the Americas. A portion of this chart is shown above.

Term to Know

vessel
a ship

Primary-Source Questions

Use your knowledge of social studies and your world history textbook to help you analyze this chart.

Constructed Response

Read each question carefully. Write your answer on the lines provided.

1. **What were the names of the German merchant vessels in Rio de Janeiro?**

   Bahia Blanca, Bollwerk, La Coruna, Minden, and *Santos*

2. **How many German ships were in port in Argentina and Brazil in 1939?**

   19

3. **Where was the largest passenger-cargo vessel docked? What was its name?**

   Bahia, Brazil; *Antonio Delfino*

4. **How many vessels were docked at Pernambuco in Brazil?**

   three

Essay

Write an essay on a separate sheet of paper. Use specific details and information from the document in your essay.

Explain why Secretary of State Sumner Welles wrote a letter to President Franklin Roosevelt listing the location of German ships in the Americas. What information could be gained from the contents of this letter?

Essay

See page xiv of this book for a scoring rubric.

The United States had to gather information about Germany because Germany was at war with nations in Europe. Secretary of State Sumner Welles reported to President Roosevelt on the location of German vessels in the Americas. The President could use the information in this letter to direct U.S. forces to seize German ships or to track German supplies or passengers if the United States went to war with Germany.

Activity

Choose a current event or historical topic that interests you. Then, draw a chart, timeline, bar graph, and circle graph that include information about your topic. Be sure to identify the subject, purpose, and date(s) in the title. Share your informational graphics with your class.

Document-Based Question

Leaders Throughout History

This test is based on the primary-source documents on pages 93–98. As you analyze the documents, take into account both the historical context, or time in history, and the point of view of each source.

Read *A Snapshot From History* to learn more about the theme of this test. Read *Background Notes* to learn more about each document.

A Snapshot From History ■ ■ ■ ■ ■ ■ ■ ■ ■ ■ ■ ■ ■ ■ ■ ■ ■ ■ ■

What qualities do great leaders possess? What are the ways that leaders bring about changes in society and other **reforms**? Throughout history, there have been many great leaders who have addressed the problems of their nations and worked hard to improve the lives of their nations' citizens. Some of these leaders protected their countries from invasion. Others used their power and influence to solve the problems of their nations.

Great leaders can bring people together, promote unity, and strengthen **nationalism**. Often, they devote their energy and power to protecting individual freedoms and beliefs. They make laws to protect citizens' rights and establish order. They rule justly and are committed to positively shaping the future of their countries. They also work responsibly to set goals, and they try to understand and meet the needs of the people.

Terms to Know

reform
  a social or political
  improvement
 	
nationalism
  devotion to one's
  nation; patriotism

Task

Using information from the following documents and your knowledge of world history, answer the questions that follow each document in Part A. Your answers to the questions will help you write the essay in Part B in which you will be asked to

◆ Discuss the contributions of at least four leaders and give examples of how each brought about positive social change.

◆ Discuss the qualities that great leaders need to possess in order to achieve their goals and make an impact on society.

PART A: CONSTRUCTED RESPONSE

Directions

Analyze the documents and answer the questions that follow each document in the space provided. Your answers to these questions will help you write an essay described on page 99.

Document 1

Background Notes

Hammurabi, ruler of Babylonia from 1792 to 1750 B.C., is most remembered for being a lawmaker. He developed a code of 282 laws that focused on family life, property rights, working conditions, and both civil and criminal issues. This code was engraved on a stone slab that survives to this day. Below is a small portion of his code.

From The Code of Hammurabi (1792–1750 B.C.)

[The gods] Anu and Bel called by name me, Hammurabi, the exalted prince . . . to bring about the rule of righteousness in the land, to destroy the wicked and the evil-doers so that the strong should not harm the weak . . . to further the well-being of mankind. . . .

5. If a judge try a case, reach a decision, and present his judgment in writing; if later error shall appear in his decision, and it be through his own fault, then he shall pay twelve times the fine set by him in the case, and he shall be publicly removed from the judge's bench, and never again shall he sit there to render judgment. . . .

21. If any one break a hole into a house [break in to steal], he shall be put to death before that hole and be buried. . . .

196. If a man puts out the eye of another man, his eye shall be put out.

---

1. Why did Hammurabi establish a code of laws for Babylonia?

The gods Anu and Bel told him to create a set of laws to punish evil-doers,

protect the weak from the strong, and "further the well-being of mankind."

2. Identify two of Hammurabi's laws.

The thief was put to death and buried in front of the house he had robbed.

If you injured someone, you would be injured in the same way.

Document 2

Background Notes

Octavian was the great-nephew and adopted son of Julius Caesar. He was named consul, or a chief official, of Rome when he was 19 years old. The Roman senate later decided that Octavian should be called Augustus Caesar. *Augustus* is a Latin word meaning "the most admired and respected."

As ruler of Rome from 44 B.C. until A.D. 14, Augustus created a system of government that stabilized the region and provided peace and prosperity. Augustus Caesar is most known for rebuilding the city of Rome and making life better for the people. Below is a portion of a description of Augustus written by Suetonius, a Roman historian.

From Suetonius, The Divine Augustus

The city [Rome], which was not built in a manner suitable to the grandeur of the empire, and was liable to inundation [flooding] of the Tiber, as well as to fires, was so much improved under his [Augustus's] administration, that he boasted, not without reason, that he found it of brick, but left it of marble.... He appointed a nightly watch to be on their guard against accidents from fire; and to prevent the frequent inundations, he widened and cleansed the bed of the Tiber.... Temples decayed by time, or destroyed by fire, he either repaired or rebuilt.... Bands of robbers... he quelled [stopped] by establishing posts of soldiers in suitable stations for the purpose; the houses of correction were subjected to a strict superintendence.... How much he was beloved for his worthy conduct in all these respects, it is easy to imagine.

3. **Describe five ways in which life in Rome was improved by Augustus.**

    Augustus made many improvements. For example, he appointed people to

    guard against fires. To help prevent flooding, he had the banks of the Tiber

    River widened and cleaned out. He had temples repaired and rebuilt.

    Soldiers were posted in the region to prevent robbers from committing

    crimes. Prisons were tightly supervised.

Document 3

Background Notes

In the early 1800s, Simón Bolívar, a statesman and soldier from South America, led revolutions against Spain to liberate what is now known as Venezuela, Colombia, Ecuador, Peru, and Bolivia.

▲ Simón Bolívar (center) and his battalion after the Battle of Carabobo, July 24, 1821

4. **What does the painting suggest about the outcome of the battle? Explain your answer.**

Bolívar and his troops look victorious. Bolívar and his men sit proudly on

their horses and do not look as if they have just lost the battle.

5. **Do you think that the artist who painted this picture was a supporter of Bolívar? Explain your answer.**

The artist was a supporter of Bolívar. He shows Bolívar, handsomely dressed,

on a white horse, leading a group of men. If the painter did not support Bolívar,

he would not show him in such a positive way.

Document 4

Background Notes

During the late 1800s, the two powerful nations of Russia and Japan were enemies. They went to war in 1904 because both countries wanted to control Korea and Manchuria. Between August and September 1905, U.S. President Theodore Roosevelt led peace talks to end the Russo-Japanese War.

▲ At Kittery, Maine, in 1905, during the Portsmouth Peace Conference, President Theodore Roosevelt ended the Russo-Japanese War, after letting Japan gain control of Korea.

6. **Describe two symbols found in the political cartoon.**

   The drum is a symbol of war. It is covered by a banner and olive branch

   that symbolize peace.

7. **How is President Roosevelt portrayed in the cartoon?**

   He is shown as the mediator because he stands between the Japanese and

   Russian leaders. He looks confident and powerful.

Document 5

Background Notes

Known as Mahatma, or "Great Soul," Mohandas Gandhi was the spiritual and political leader of India. As head of the Indian National Congress, he gave speeches arguing that Great Britain should leave India. The people of India no longer wanted the British to maintain political, social, and economic control over their country.

From Mohandas Gandhi, The Quit India Speeches (1942)

Ours is not a drive for power, but purely a nonviolent fight for India's independence.... A nonviolent soldier of freedom will covet [want] nothing for himself, he fights only for the freedom of his country. The Congress is unconcerned as to who will rule, when freedom is attained. The power, when it comes, will belong to the people of India, and it will be for them to decide to whom it placed in the entrusted....

Our quarrel is not with the British people, we fight their imperialism. The proposal for the withdrawal of British power did not come out of anger. It came to enable India to play its due part at the present critical juncture [World War II]....

Here is a *mantra* [saying] a short one, that I give you.... The *mantra* is "Do or die." We shall either free India or die in the attempt; we shall not live to see the perpetuation [continuation] of our slavery. Every true Congressman or woman will join the struggle with an inflexible determination not to remain alive to see the country in bondage and slavery. Let that be your pledge.

8. Who does Gandhi want to rule India when it becomes a free nation?

Gandhi is not concerned about who will rule a free India. He believes the

people will make that decision.

9. What does the phrase "Do or die" mean?

It means that Gandhi and the other members of the Indian National Congress

will either free India or die while attempting to do so.

Document 6

Background Notes

Nelson Mandela was one of the leaders of the African National Congress (ANC) and president of South Africa from 1994 to 1999. Mandela was successful in helping to end apartheid, the policy of racial separation and discrimination in South Africa.

▲ In 1994, Nelson Mandela (left) was the ANC's candidate in the South African presidential election. This was the first democratic, all-race election held in South Africa.

10. Describe what can be learned about the 1994 presidential election in South Africa from the photograph.

The election was a joyous occasion for Nelson Mandela and his supporters.

He is smiling as he casts his vote. His supporters stand behind him and one

proudly waves a flag. The photograph also tells us that black Africans were

able to vote. Finally, ballots were cast by hand and placed in a box. So,

high-tech voting machines were not used.

PART B: ESSAY

Directions

- ◆ Write a well-organized essay that includes an introduction, several paragraphs, and a conclusion.

- ◆ Support your response with relevant facts, examples, and details from at least four primary-source documents.

- ◆ Include specific, related outside information.

- ◆ Use the three-column chart below to help plan your essay.

Essay

Using your answers and notes from Part A and your knowledge of world history, write an essay on a separate sheet of paper in which you

- ◆ Discuss the contributions of at least four leaders and give examples of how each brought about positive social change.

- ◆ Discuss the qualities that great leaders need to possess in order to achieve their goals and make an impact on society.

Essay
See page xiii of this book for a sample essay and page xiv for a scoring rubric.

Contributions and Qualities of Leaders		
Leader	**Contributions**	**Qualities**
Hammurabi	Created a set of laws to help protect the rights and well-being of his people; established a way to govern his region	Fair and just; rational; ethical
Augustus	Reorganized Roman life; made many improvements, such as repairing and rebuilding temples	Effective administrator; organized; knowledgeable; capable
Simón Bolívar	Led revolutions against Spain to liberate South American colonies	Courageous; strong; decisive; commanding
Theodore Roosevelt	Negotiated agreement that ended Russo-Japanese War	Courageous; strong; smart politician; mediator; peacemaker
Mohandas Gandhi	Fought nonviolently for India's independence; campaigned to bring about change	Spiritual; inspirational; nonviolent; unselfish; moral; truthful
Nelson Mandela	Helped to end apartheid; improved life for black South Africans; fought for human rights	Determined; committed; effective

Document-Based Question

Human Migration

This test is based on the primary-source documents on pages 101–106. As you analyze the documents, take into account both the historical context, or time in history, and the point of view of each source.

Read *A Snapshot From History* to learn more about the theme of this test. Read *Background Notes* to learn more about each document.

A Snapshot From History ▪▪▪▪▪▪▪▪▪▪▪▪▪▪▪

The permanent change in residence of large groups of people, called **migration**, has occurred throughout history. People migrate for different reasons. They immigrate to other countries, leaving their homes for economic, social, or political reasons. Some people continually move around looking for work, such as agricultural workers. They change residence when crops are being harvested in different locations, then return to a home base when their work is done. Nomads, with no permanent residence, sometimes travel in order to move herds to fresh grazing grounds.

Forced migrations have also occurred throughout history—and still continue in parts of the world today. For example, from the sixteenth century through the nineteenth century, approximately 20 million enslaved Africans were forcibly sent to the Americas and the West Indies.

Forced migrations are often the results of wars. In Germany during the 1940s, between 7 and 8 million people were deported, or sent away, including approximately 6 million Jews. In 2002, hundreds of thousands of people from the African nation of Sierra Leone were **refugees** as a result of 10 years of civil war.

Terms to Know

migration
movement from one place to another

refugee
a person who leaves his or her homeland because of war or persecution

Task

Using information from the following documents and your knowledge of world history, answer the questions that follow each document in Part A. Your answers to the questions will help you write the essay in Part B in which you will be asked to

◆ Discuss the social, political, and economic reasons for human migration.

◆ Provide examples of migration throughout world history.

PART A: CONSTRUCTED RESPONSE

Directions

Analyze the documents and answer the questions that follow each document in the space provided. Your answers to these questions will help you write an essay described on page 107.

Document 1

Background Notes

During the Ice Age more than 30,000 years ago, ice covered huge sections of Earth's surface. Sea levels were lower, so more land was exposed, connecting continents that are separated by seas today. Some scientists believe that humans and animals migrated across land bridges and settled throughout the world. As the ice melted over time, the oceans rose and the land bridges were covered by water.

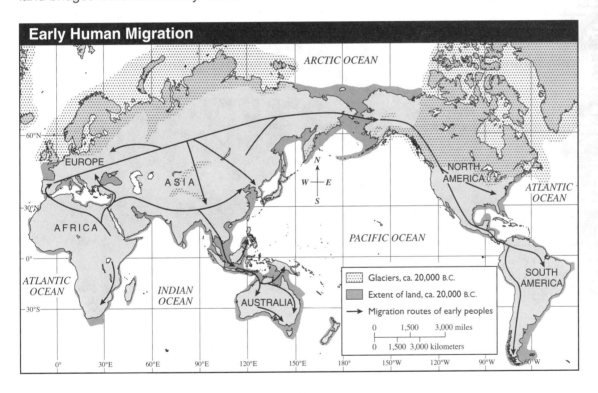

Early Human Migration

1. **From which continent did early human migration originate?**

   Africa

2. **To which continents were people able to migrate as a result of crossing land bridges?**

   from Africa to Europe; from Asia to North America; and from Asia to Australia

101

Document 2

Background Notes

The Silk Road was an ancient trade route, 4,000 miles long, that came into existence in the early second century B.C. It linked China with the West, enabling people to transport goods and ideas back and forth. Caravans, or groups of merchants traveling together, carried valuable Chinese silk westward. Goods like silver and gold were transported to the East.

▲ The ancient Tang city of Gaochang (above) was a military and supply center on the Silk Road. The Silk Road can be seen in front of the city's ruins. Caravan merchants (right) traveled the Silk Road on camels.

3. **Use the photograph and the artifact to describe conditions for travelers on the ancient Silk Road.**

    The road was rocky and passed through rugged lands, including

    mountainous and desert areas. Merchants had to carry all of their goods

    and supplies for the journey with them as they traveled by camel. They

    probably did not travel far in one day.

Document 3

Background Notes

In the ninth and tenth centuries, warriors from Scandinavia, called Vikings, raided European coastal towns and villages. These seafaring warriors sometimes burned villages, robbing and killing the inhabitants. Due to overpopulation in their homelands and weak opponents in Europe, the Vikings colonized large sections of Europe during this time.

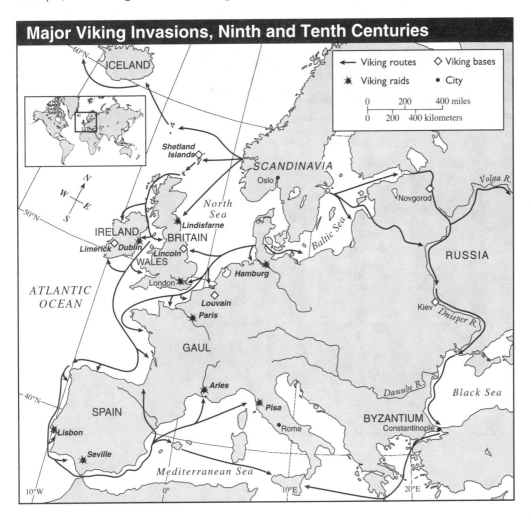

Major Viking Invasions, Ninth and Tenth Centuries

4. **Describe the route used by the Vikings to reach the city of Constantinople from Scandinavia.**

   Vikings crossed Baltic Sea, and some passed Novgorod. Then, they followed the

   Dnieper River south, passed Kiev, and sailed the Black Sea to Constantinople.

5. **Where was the most southern Viking raid and how far was it from Scandinavia by boat?**

   Seville; about 2,600 miles

Document 4

Background Notes

Immigrants from around the world have come to the United States for economic opportunities as well as to escape religious and political persecution. In the 1840s, many Europeans emigrated to North America from Ireland and Germany. This was due to famine and the failure of the potato crop in Ireland, which was that country's primary source of food. In the 1880s, a larger migration occurred from eastern Europe and southern Europe, again for agricultural reasons.

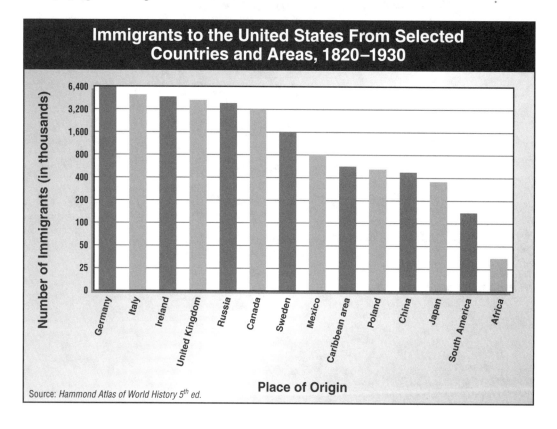

Immigrants to the United States From Selected Countries and Areas, 1820–1930

Source: *Hammond Atlas of World History 5th ed.*

6. **How many years does this graph cover?**

   110 years

7. **Which country had the third largest number of people emigrating to the United States? Why might they have emigrated?**

   Ireland; they were starving because the potato crop failed, which was their

   primary food source.

Document 5

Background Notes

On November 29, 1947, British-ruled Palestine in the Middle East was divided into Jewish and Arab states by the United Nations. Fighting immediately broke out because the Arabs opposed the decision. On May 14, 1948, Israel's National Council wrote a declaration of independence that was supported by the United States, the Soviet Union, and many other world governments. Below is a portion of the declaration.

From Ben-Gurion, Declaration of Israel's Independence (1948)

The land of Israel was the birthplace of the Jewish people. Here their spiritual, religious and national identity was formed. Here they achieved independence and created a culture of national and universal significance. . . .

Exiled from Palestine, the Jewish people remained faithful to it in all the countries of their dispersion [scattering], never ceasing to pray and hope for their return and the restoration of their national freedom. . . .

The Nazi holocaust, which engulfed millions of Jews in Europe, proved anew the urgency of the re-establishment of the Jewish state, which would solve the problem of Jewish homelessness by opening the gates to all Jews and lifting the Jewish people to equality in the family of nations.

The survivors of the European catastrophe, as well as Jews from other lands, proclaiming their right to a life of dignity, freedom and labor, and undeterred [not stopped] by hazards, hardships and obstacles, have tried unceasingly to enter Palestine. . . .

We, the members of the National Council . . . hereby proclaim the establishment of the Jewish State in Palestine, to be called Israel.

8. **Why did Israel want to form a Jewish State in Palestine?**

The land of Israel was the birthplace of the Jewish people. Because they were

exiled, or forced to leave their homeland, they wanted to return. In addition, the

Nazi holocaust caused the deaths of millions of Jews and left many homeless.

These survivors, as well as other Jews from around the world, wanted to live

a life of dignity and freedom in a land they could call their own.

Document 6

Background Notes

Somalia is located in the easternmost part of Africa. Its capital city is Mogadishu. By 1991, the country was in a state of anarchy, or total confusion. Civil war among different groups had devastated the country, killing many Somalis, destroying cities, and collapsing the economy. Many Somalis were starving, had lost their homes, and were living in fear. Below is a portion of an account written by a teenager, Ayan, who fled from Somalia in 1997.

From Ayan, "Long Journey to the United States" (1997)

I was born in Mogadishu. I lived there all my life until my family left. Before the civil war, my life was normal. I went to school and lived with my family.

I left Somalia in 1991 with my mother and younger brother. We left because of the civil war. We were afraid for our lives. Somalia was not safe. Gangs would break into houses during the night. They would either rob or kill civilians, most of whom had no weapons. It was common to see dead people lying in the streets of Mogadishu.... The war had a serious effect on me personally because I lost some of my classmates in the fighting. They were with their families and planned to get out of the city until the tensions eased. But they never made it out. They were killed before they could leave.... One day my mother decided that we had to leave Somalia.... We left all my relatives behind—uncles, aunts, and grandmother. On our way out of Somalia, we stayed at several places in the country: first Qoryoley, then Kismayu. Wherever we went we saw violence and war. Finally we left the country and went to a refugee camp in Kenya. The United Nations helped us to resettle and register in the camp.

I was unhappy for the first few days. The camp was very hot and overcrowded. It was difficult to get water or food. We had to stand in a long line for many hours. Also, the camp was not safe.... Finally, at the end of 1993, I left Kenya for the United States.... I want to help my country in the future. Someday I will visit it when these problems are worked out. I can't forget my country.

9. **Why did Ayan and her family leave Somalia and come to the United States?**

Years of civil war made the city of Mogadishu where Ayan and her family lived

unsafe. They were afraid of the gangs that broke into houses to rob or kill

civilians. Some of Ayan's classmates were even killed.

PART B: ESSAY

Directions

- Write a well-organized essay that includes an introduction, several paragraphs, and a conclusion.

- Support your response with relevant facts, examples, and details from at least four primary-source documents.

- Include specific, related outside information.

- Use the idea web below to help plan your essay.

Essay

Using your answers and notes from Part A and your knowledge of world history, write an essay on a separate sheet of paper in which you

- Discuss the social, political, and economic reasons for human migration.

- Provide examples of migration throughout world history.

Essay
See page xiii of this book for a sample essay and page xiv for a scoring rubric.

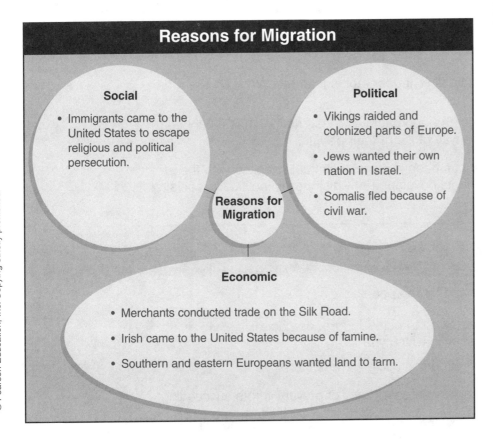

Reasons for Migration

Social
- Immigrants came to the United States to escape religious and political persecution.

Political
- Vikings raided and colonized parts of Europe.
- Jews wanted their own nation in Israel.
- Somalis fled because of civil war.

Reasons for Migration

Economic
- Merchants conducted trade on the Silk Road.
- Irish came to the United States because of famine.
- Southern and eastern Europeans wanted land to farm.

Document-Based Question Essay Topics

Listed below are topics that you can use to practice writing essays. Your essay should include examples from primary sources that support the main idea.

Essay 1: Revolution

Throughout history, many revolutions have been fought due to political, economic, and social unrest. These revolutions have impacted governments and societies and led to many changes.

Task: Choose one revolution from world history. Write an essay in which you

- Explain the causes of the revolution.

- Explain the effects of the revolution.

- Evaluate whether or not the revolution resolved significant problems of the time.

Essay 2: Geography and Its Impact on Society

The geography of a place impacts, or influences, its development. Location, environment, and availability of resources have impacted countries in a variety of ways.

Task: Choose two countries with different geographic features. Write an essay in which you

- Compare and contrast how the geography of these nations has influenced their development and the way of life of their people.

- Determine which country has been more successful in dealing with the effect that geography has had on its development—historically, politically, socially, and economically.

Essay 3: Democracy

Democracy is a government by and for the people.

Task: Choose three nations that have struggled to form democratic governments. Write an essay in which you

- Explain common practices of democratic governments.

- Describe conditions that can help a democracy or prevent it from succeeding.

- Give specific examples of how three nations have succeeded in forming a democracy.

Glossary

A

absolute monarch a ruler who is not limited by laws or a constitution (p. 24)

aqueduct a system of pipes and bridges used to carry water long distances (p. 12)

aviation the science or art of operating and navigating aircraft (p. 52)

B

bargaining agent a person who tries to make an agreement between two parties (p. 50)

C

capitalism an economic system based on the investment of money in businesses for profit (p. 26)

censorship the policy of banning objectionable materials, such as books or newspapers (p. 18)

citadel a fort that commands a city (p. 69)

civil war war between groups of people from the same country (p. 62)

code a set of laws (p. 12)

colony a settlement in a distant land that is governed by another country (p. 88)

commerce trade; the buying and selling of goods (p. 76)

conquistador the Spanish term for *conqueror*, or one who gains control by winning a war (p. 38)

consul a high-ranking government official (p. 21)

contract a legally binding agreement (p. 14)

counterrevolutionary working against a government set up by a previous revolution (p. 54)

czar the Russian word for *Caesar*, which means "emperor" (p 24)

D

democracy a government that gives its citizens the ruling power (p. 54)

demographer a social scientist who studies population trends (p. 81)

developing country a country in which industrialization is still taking place (p. 81)

dictator a ruler of a government who has absolute power (p. 18)

diplomacy negotiations or discussions between countries (p. 30)

dynasty a group of rulers who all belong to the same family (p. 40)

E

Enlightenment the eighteenth-century movement when thinkers believed they could logically explain human nature (p. 14)

export goods sent out of a country to be sold in another country (p. 16)

F

fortress an enclosed place used for military defense (p. 74)

Führer leader (p. 45)

H

hieroglyphics picture writing (p. 38)

hijra the flight of Muhammad and his followers from Mecca to Medina in 622 (p. 72)

human rights the basic freedoms that all people should have (p. 9)

I

immigrant a person who enters a new country to live there (p. 76)

Industrial Revolution beginning in Great Britain in the mid-1700s, the shift from making goods by hand to using power-driven machines (p. 42)

J

jurisdiction an area of authority (p. 9)

L

labor union an association of workers that protects the interests of its members (p. 50)

M

Middle Passage the second leg of the triangular trade routes in which slaves were shipped across the Atlantic Ocean (p. 86)

migration movement from one place to another (p. 100)

minerals substances obtained by mining (p. 78)

mortality rates death rates (p. 81)

mural a picture painted directly on a wall (p. 64)

N

nationalism devotion to one's nation; patriotism (p. 92)

natural resources materials supplied by nature that are useful to people (p. 78)

O

oral history the history of a people that is told by storytellers (p. 36)

P

pharaoh a title given to the rulers of ancient Egypt (p. 48)

port a city or town where ships can load and unload cargo (p. 74)

propaganda the promotion of certain ideas to influence people's opinions (p. 45)

pyramid a large structure with a square base and triangular sides that meet in a point at the top (p. 57)

R

reform a social or political improvement (p. 92)

refugee a person who leaves his or her homeland because of war or persecution (p. 100)

regime a government (p. 50)

S

samurai a Japanese warrior (p. 66)

secede to withdraw or leave (p. 62)

shogun the supreme military commander of Japan (p. 66)

socialism an economic system in which the means of production are collectively owned or owned by the government (p. 26)

socialist market economy an economic system that blends features of socialism with features of capitalism (p. 26)

subcontinent a large part of a continent that is geographically separated from the rest of the continent (p. 69)

T

terrorism the use of threats, force, or acts of violence to frighten governments or people to change their policies (p. 28)

textile cloth manufactured from wool, cotton, or other materials (p. 69)

textile industry the manufacturing of cloth from wool, cotton, and other materials (p. 42)

treaty a formal agreement between two or more nations (p. 16)

triangular trade a trading system involving a three-way exchange of goods and people in Europe, Africa, and the Americas (p. 86)

tribute payment given by one nation to another more powerful nation; may be paid in exchange for protection (p. 84)

V

vessel a ship (p. 90)

Index